teach yourself

marketing

teach® yourself

marketing
j jonathan gabay

For UK order queries: please contact Bookpoint Ltd, 130 Milton Park, Abingdon, Oxon OX14 4SB. Telephone: (44) 01235 827720. Fax: (44) 01235 400454. Lines are open from 9.00–18.00, Monday to Saturday, with a 24-hour message answering service. Email address: orders@bookpoint.co.uk

For U.S.A. order queries: please contact McGraw-Hill Customer Services, P.O. Box 545, Blacklick, OH 43004-0545, U.S.A. Telephone: 1-800-722-4726. Fax: 1-614-755-5645.

For Canada order queries: please contact McGraw-Hill Ryerson Ltd, 300 Water St, Whitby, Ontario L1N 9B6, Canada. Telephone: 905 430 5000. Fax: 905 430 5020.

Long-renowned as the authoritative source for self-guided learning – with more than 30 million copies sold worldwide – the *Teach Yourself* series includes over 300 titles in the fields of languages, crafts, hobbies, business and education.

A catalogue entry for this title is available from The British Library.

Library of Congress Catalog Card Number: on file

First published in UK 1995 by Contemporary Books, A Division of the McGraw-Hill Companies, 4255 West Touhy Avenue, Lincolnwood (Chicago), Illinois 60646 – 1975 U.S.A.

This edition published 2003.

The 'Teach Yourself' name and logo are registered trade marks of Hodder & Stoughton Ltd.

Typeset by Transet Limited, Coventry, England.
Printed in Great Britain for Hodder & Stoughton Educational, a division of Hodder Headline Ltd, 338 Euston Road, London NW1 3BH by Cox & Wyman Ltd, Reading, Berkshire.

Impression number	7 6 5 4 3 2 1
Year	2007 2006 2005 2004 2003

contents

Dedication

For everyone who ever had the guts to ask why not?

Special thanks to: Maurice Berrzimra, Michelle, Joshua – and, of course, the distinguished contributors.

also

Katie Roden

Open your eyes to opportunities
Open your mind to imagination
and the world opens to you

About the author

Jonathan Gabay describes himself as a person who wears lots of hats. In addition to writing books, he lectures on marketing, copywriting and creative advertising and is a regular speaker at international events. He also runs a creative boutique – Gabay. It specializes in value-added, innovative, through-the-line creative solutions for marketers wishing to secure and sustain a top-of-mind positioning in an already established market.

Jonathan's copywriting is award winning. His books include the best-selling *Teach Yourself Copywriting* – published by Hodder and Stoughton, *Successful Webmarketing in a Week* (Hodder Headline, 2002), *Reinvent Yourself* (Momentum, 2002) and the highly successful *Meaning of Life* (Virgin Publishing, 1995). His work is published in the United Kingdom, United States, Canada and Australia. He has also been translated into Japanese and Taiwanese.

When not working, he values time with his family from whom he draws inspiration, courage and love – everything else, he's keeping under his hat.

beyond your wildest imagination

Beyond your wildest imagination lies a place called 'opportunity' – welcome!

Imagination is the natural opium of the mind. The world of imaginative marketing steps beyond the normal parameters of traditional marketing. It enters an unlimited dimension.

Whatever the size and type of your organization, this book will help to confirm marketing as the fastest developing of all business tools. In addition to explaining key marketing techniques supported by interviews with leading authorities, I'll discuss the origins and significance of some of the most fascinating areas in the field of marketing.

Marketing is neither convoluted nor academic. It's about real life; getting the most out of relationships. To maximize those relationships, we'll uncover the crucial issues you need to know from unfolding classic marketing fundamentals to stretching your marketing budget without squeezing its effect. There are also insights on brands – *for example, Chrysler was so named in 1923 after American engineer Walter Percy Chrysler*, and much more besides. In fact, I'll reveal marketing techniques used by some of the world's most powerful organizations – ready for you to adapt and adopt.

Throughout, **Marking in action** exercises put you to the test.

Eager to explore *your* potential, exploit further your own abilities, the marketing function of your organization and, not least, your target audience? Then driven by the momentum of your imagination, like toppling dominoes, one by one I'll guide you towards generating maximum impact in your marketplace.

J. Jonathan Gabay
JJ@gabaynet.com

01

the tools
of the trade

In this chapter you will learn about:
- the roots of marketing
- the Boston matrix
- product life cycles
- classic marketing formulae
- global markets

Marketing is not just advertising or selling – although both form part of the process. Unless you make it otherwise, marketing isn't complicated. Sun Tzu, the fourth-century Chinese military strategist said, '*the most difficult things in the world must be done while they are still easy*'. Open the marketing kit of simple business tools and you'll find four neatly divided sections, each featuring distinctive processes:

1 Strategic marketing analysis
2 Communications planning
3 Marketing implementation
4 Marketing control.

The essence of marketing is understanding, supporting, appreciating and being sympathetic towards people connected with your organization. Just as a river meanders, so your marketing adapts and blends into a commercial landscape.

Understanding target audience motivation requires imaginative foresight. This issue affects every type of business – for example and of particular relevance to this book, marketing training. David Thorp, Training Development Director at one of the UK's most innovative marketing educational centres, the Chartered Institute of Marketing, explains:

> Learning in marketing means on-going development of individual talents. On our part that takes consistent commitment to clients. In today's complex business environment, keeping in tune with needs means having the broadest possible perspective of training trends in other disciplines. This is where market leading customer care, consistent quality – in every thing we do, up-to-the-minute innovative educational standards and so imaginative marketing really comes into its own.

Often, marketing books get really hung up on the minutiae of the marketing process. Such details are important and I'll explain more as you progress through this book. Meanwhile, bear in mind that the main objective is to aim higher – that is, getting along profitably with the people working by your side as, indeed, with future investors in your products, services and business.

Iceberg ahead!

There is a marketing lesson to be learned from the tragedy that befell the cruise liner *Titanic*. The key issue was the hidden depths of the deadly iceberg. Urged to make 'marketing' headlines, the ship's captain, Edward J. Smith, ordered *full steam ahead* to reach New York in record time. The ship had received a total of seven iceberg warnings. But the sea was calm and the Officer of the Bridge, William Murdoch, decided eyesight rather than foresight would suffice.

Marketing is about getting things right by keeping a watchful eye on the horizon as well as an ear to what's happening below, around as well as above the 'deck' of your business. Approaching midnight on 14 April 1912, a mountainous iceberg was spotted and Murdoch desperately tried to turn the ship around. His action was in vain. The iceberg gnawed a row of gaping tooth marks into the ship's structure. Within two hours, along with its invincible promises, the 'unsinkable' *Titanic* sunk.

Only 20 lifeboats were on board. The wives and children of dignitaries were saved first. Over 1,500 men, women and children perished. The marketing lesson? Protocol comes second to marketplace vigilance to enable those in charge to protect and safeguard those in your care.

The evolution of marketing

Marketing forms part of the process of exchange. That is, giving up something in return for something else which has some perceived value. Humankind's original idea of supply and demand was pretty much a self-centred affair. The hunter made a crude weapon to kill an animal. If a vessel was needed to carry the food, the hunter improvised. Then came the task of gathering wood for a fire. Once again, someone had to come up with the goods. So it was that humankind floated along in this lonely, *self-sufficient* existence, getting nowhere fast. Instead of clobbering as many wild boar as possible, the hunter spent energy and time dealing with related aspects. The same could be said for the people who could have been profitably concentrating on their own jobs such as flint sharpening or wood gathering. There had to be a better solution. So the process of *decentralized exchange* was evolved. In this economy, the hunter, the flint maker, the wood gatherer and the rest of the clan started to see each other in a different light. Each was a potential buyer. Collectively, they formed a *market*.

The hunter's life became more structured. After a good day's clobbering, the hunter visited suppliers to trade the best rump steak. Everything seemed to progress reasonably well. Yet, think about it; after ambushing wild boar all day, would *you* really want to drag a carcass around, calling on different traders?

Enter the *merchant* who established a centralized *marketplace*. Along with the other hunters, the hunter brought meat to the merchant who acted as a catalyst for the exchange of services and goods. So the hunter established a profitable point of contact, dealt with the market as a whole and even gained time to clobber bigger game.

This formed a solid foundation for a market in which:

1 'Producers' could assess the value of their goods or services.
2 Buyers knew what they were prepared to exchange for those goods or services.
3 For a percentage of the transaction, merchants acted as intermediaries between established or likely buyers and sellers.

The marketplace's profitable reputation grew. Further deals were struck. Specialist merchants traded in particular items. New markets developed. Humankind evolved, so did its needs. Eventually there were all kinds of markets including job markets, money markets, commodity markets and, most recently, futures markets.

There have always been several options for exchange. Our hunter bartered meat and could also have offered time and experience. Once a value of some goods has been established and a currency of exchange agreed, each of the parties has the choice either to accept or refuse the proposed 'trade'. Finally, they need skills to communicate what they want, when they want it and how it will be delivered. (*See also*, 'Tribal branding', page 181).

The 'now' age

Today, sellers and buyers don't always meet face to face. Merchants transport goods anywhere. Distribution has embraced the World Wide Web. E-mail has altered the classical hierarchy of an organization. Even the sound of money has changed from the *chingle* of loose change to the '*click, hum and swipe*' of electronic gadgetry and smart cards. Nationwide, Europewide or worldwide, imaginative marketing lifts products off a page, website and, of course, shelf. Cell phones, web pages and PDAS can record the golden digits of your credit card. Sophisticated stock control technology moves goods out of a warehouse, whilst delivery services, supported by ingenious stock database technology, places them into a customer's hand.

It is an economy where anything, including the bones of extinct prehistoric creatures, has its place, price and market.

What is marketing?

An organization's most influential and creative business tool is marketing. Like any powerful instrument, it needs to be constantly reviewed, preened and prepared to meet new challenges.

Danielle Aarons, one of Australia's leading marketers, explains:

> Marketing managers must become business managers controlling a portfolio of goods and services to maximize profit and revenue. That's tough in a competitive market with few opportunities to hold a unique point of difference for long.
>
> (*See also* 'USPs' in 'Under the microscope', page 143).

Marketing isn't black and white

Economists tend to view marketing from a black-and-white sales perspective (as if the sales process was that easily defined). Generally speaking, neo-classical economic theory is led by supply and demand considerations. Most economists would argue that if costs could be reduced sufficiently to benefit consumers, demand for a product or service would follow.

But if that was the case, your only tool would be a series of cost reduction exercises. In a competitive arena, where High Noon is marked by the player still left standing after a trade shoot-out, either you or your competitor would eventually be fired out of business.

Four unfocused views on marketing

The Financial Director

'Do it by the book. Avoid risks. Look at previous research to confirm you are on track and the rest will look after itself.'

The Department Head

'Save money, just add another department. Offer a standardized customer service function. Who cares about expensive specialists?'

The Sales Director

'It's all sales. If you can't sell now, cut the price, sell high later. *Trust me on this.*'

The Chief Executive

'"Arty" marketing ideas and fine salespeople are wonderful, providing you make me and the shareholders a dollar, pound or euro, and make it snappy.'

Whenever one person succeeds, another comes close second (Early industrial marketing)

During the late nineteenth-century industrial boom period, the pure, economic theory of marketing was at its most practical. You name it, someone wanted it. As long as you could produce enough, the chances were pretty good that someone, somewhere would buy it. And if the going got tough – you reduced costs.

As the manufacturing process became more sophisticated, product variations became more extensive. This led to increased product-range competition. When product variations ran out of drawing-board space, it was back to cutting prices. Sooner or later, companies could no longer sustain the reductions. As they couldn't slice sales prices, they cut the cost of manufacturing. Companies became more efficient in production techniques. It was an era of time-and-motion studies. Lower production costs led to greater output and keener prices.

Driven by market demands, the wheels of industry again turned out profits. Service, too, began to play an important part, starting with a salesperson and ending with after-sales care.

Keeping the customers satisfied

Everything about marketing evolves around satisfying the consumer. By identifying needs you can look at ways to make your service or product attractive, appealing and relevant. That secures sales. However, sales don't even get off the ground without some kind of promotion. When used intelligently, advertising convinces consumers and persuades them to alter buying patterns and behaviour. By doing so, marketers assume the roles of commercial cupids – nurturing long-term relationships between the customer and a brand.

However, this puts the kibosh on the purely economic-led view of marketing. After all, some economists consider one of the roles of advertising is to help consumers save time and costs when choosing a product or service.

Value generates demand. This, in turn, influences price. Look at it subjectively. If you endow enough attributes to a product or service through targeting a defined market, you address a multitude of discernible values, including:

- product and service
- quality
- social
- image.

So, potentially, markets are not just rationally led: but subjectively and even emotionally motivated. A good example of the latter is the perfume business which addresses feelings rather than rationality. Scent may be positioned to make you feel confident, sensual or chic.

All products and services need personalities to help make them distinctive and so establish a Unique Selling Proposition (USP). (See page 143.) As the marketplace in general becomes more crowded so, like in a gigantic rave party, the individual brands with distinctive personalities will be those which make the biggest impact.

It is all a matter of positioning to influence the way consumers think and feel. (*See* 'Image is everything', page 146). Effective brand positioning which addresses customer expectations drives the marketing process forward. Once a positioning has been defined and developed, all the intrinsic and extrinsic attributes of the brand amalgamate. Later I'll elaborate on brand positioning. For now, consider a radio interview I heard. A major drinks company planned to merge with its competitor. The interviewer asked the respective chairmen to place a value on each other's companies. They concluded that the greatest value was that of the portfolio of brands.

Branding gives companies the edge over the competition. Consumers search for products and services which initially may be more expensive than a competitor's. Yet, in terms of relevance to longer-term personal aspirations and needs, these products and services deliver greater value.

Marketing in action
What is neo-classical economic theory?

Implementing the marketing plan

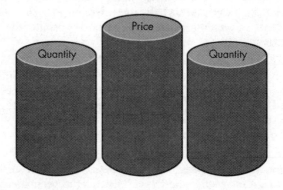

Economically, sell enough at the right price and eventually you'll reach profit targets

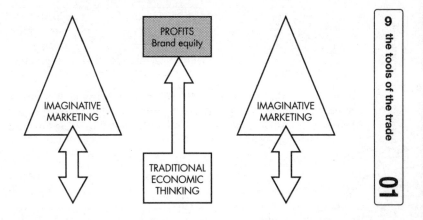

Complement economic thinking with imaginative marketing and you'll spend less time and fewer resources increasing profits and brand values

Look it up: more definitions of marketing

According to the *Oxford Concise Dictionary of Business*:

> Marketing is the process of identifying, maximizing and satisfying consumer demand for a company's products. Marketing a product involves such tasks as anticipating changes in demand (usually on the basis of market research), promotion of the product, ensuring that its quality, availability and prices meet the needs of the market and providing after-sales service.

Demand management

Marketing – as defined by Chartered Institute of Marketing:

> The management process responsible for identifying, anticipating and satisfying customer requirements profitably.

That's excellent, as long as you also accept that different organizations have different expectations from their marketing programmes. For example, charities don't make profits so they could trade the word 'profitably' for 'effectively'. (Providing you are not 'hung up' on grammatical issues like splitting your infinitives!)

> **Did you know?**
> According to the Plain English Campaign you can start a sentence with And, But, However, So. You can also split infinitives.

Your role isn't just to sell. It includes identifying a demand through research, distribution of your product or service and developing your customer base by continually looking for new ways to satisfy needs.

As an essential business process for the third millennium, part of the function of imagination-led marketing is to formulate targeted strategies which attract an audience for a particular product or service. It's down to you to probe, plan, implement and direct commercial programmes between your organization and the marketplace. In doing so, you can prosper and sustain mutually beneficial trade. (*See also* 'Iceberg ahead!', page 2).

Peter Drucker, one of the modern-day sales and marketing gurus, explains that

> ...marketing is the whole business seen from the point of view of its final result, that is, from the consumers' point of view.

Marketing – as defined by the American Marketing Association:

> The performance of a business's activities that directs the flow of goods and services from producer to consumer or user.

Marketing is not just lavishing people with what they want by anticipating, meeting and exceeding their expectations. Like a scrumptious meal, there are times when people can have too much, becoming overwhelmed with a product or service.

For example, faddish pop bands often endorse so many products that people become exposed to pop fatigue. (As Confucius said, 'To go beyond is as wrong as to fall short'.)

Demarketing – The more you twist it, the more it turns people on

Imaginative marketing management can be likened to a tap adjusting the flow of marketing techniques.

Effective imaginative marketers deal with varying levels of supply and demand. Sometimes the demand is little more than a trickle. At other times it can be torrential. Sometimes, though rarely, demand becomes too great. *Demarketing* discourages the consumer from buying or consuming something rather than stimulating him or her to do so. A typical example is when people are asked not to hose the garden during a drought.

Of course, companies are not in the business of discouraging people from using their products or services. This said, adjusting your marketing programme pays dividends. For example, in the pop music industry, a commonly used marketing technique is to publicize an album up to five weeks prior to release. You build interest leading to demand, but still there is no product on the market. Then, just when you have your eye on the top slot in the charts, you release the album and hopefully everyone buys. If not, you could always send people out to buy albums from key shops where chart sales are checked. However, although this practice has been known to be used in the record business, it is illegal, verging on the verge of fraudulent.

Did you know?
Months before a commercial is broadcast, television advertisers negotiate with record companies for marketing tie-ins with a music theme to be featured in the commercial. However, just because the product does well out of the association, it doesn't necessarily follow that the pop band will be a hit, too.

Marketing in action
List five reasons for demarketing.

A little tickle in the right place makes for a happy Tinky Winky

At the start of 1997, the BBC planned to help aliens take over the world and in doing so created the ancestors of *Bob the Builder* and *The Tweenies*. A shrewd PR and marketing campaign was hatched to introduce children to a group of cuddly creatures called Teletubbies. The characters were slightly slow on the uptake to understand concepts. This made them particularly attractive to the younger audience because they would invariably be able to grasp concepts faster than the loveable characters. This made them feel that they were in charge of the brood of Tubbies, like parents are in charge of the children. By the autumn, following the success of the

Teletubbies programme made by Ragdoll, an independent production company, a children's magazine was launched. Thus ensued a trade marketing campaign embracing *Teletubbies* videos, books and, best of all, toys.

In the run up to Christmas 1997, there appeared to be a calculated lack of toy Teletubbies in Britain. For some 12 weeks prior to Christmas, the BBC ran daily programmes featuring the Teletubby characters – Tinky Winky, Laa Laa, Po and Dipsy. Audience figures swelled to around 2 million per day.

Two months before Christmas, the BBC further promoted the Teletubby dolls through adverts and posters, the latter being seen by parents taking their children to school. Each working-day morning, *Teletubbies* programmes were broadcast just before the target audience – children aged well under 10 years – went to school. Whilst preparing breakfast, parents also watched *Teletubbies*. Soon a cult following grew, comprising adults and children.

The British went Teletubby mad. Would the children have a Teletubby for Christmas? Amid tough security, supermarket staff worked in the dead of night to stock the treasured Teletubbies. The toys were transported in unmarked vans to Brent Cross shopping mall in London, Anniesland in Glasgow and Leicester.

The Tubbies were kept under 24-hour surveillance. Ticket queuing systems were set up in anticipation of a scramble when doors opened in the morning. Meanwhile people whispered in hushed tones about their chances of getting hold of Teletubbies from unnamed underground sources – for a price. It was widely reported that a mother had placed a £1,000 ($1,400) price-tag on the heads of her son's Teletubbies. (An original doll cost her £45.96 – $64.18.) Within one day she received an offer of £500 ($700).

The BBC also released a record of the *Teletubbies* television theme tune. It reached the number one slot in the charts overnight, opening the floodgates for the dolls. A brilliant piece of imaginative marketing which left toy and CD shelves empty, store keepers delighted and BBC Enterprises wiser – ideal when years later they would use the lessons to market the likes of *The Tweenies* and *Fimbles*.

In the first 15 months, the Teletubbies made the BBC a profit of £23 million ($32 million). The Teletubbies made their US television debut on the PBS network in April 1998.

The SAS of the corporate army

One man with an idea is worth a thousand armies. Imaginative marketing co-ordinates troops of resources to meet the demands of people for products and services. Through orchestrating the process by which an organization presents its goods, it becomes armed with compelling reasons for people to choose an organization's product or service in preference to any other. Later, in greater length, we will consider these targeting issues.

Money can buy you love

Marketing first really became universally recognized as a business tool in the 1950s. By the 1960s, style and fashion were as accessible as switching on a television or listening to a portable record player. Hollywood 'went for broke' with bigger, more colourful as well as more socially 'aware' docu-dramas. Presentation was everything. The marketing man was a showman, more interested in 'shine' than product substance.

> Any monopoly, including the brand, is bad
>
> Adam Smith

The swinging Seventies

The 1970s shook the world into uncomfortable reality. The climate was intemperate. Political scandals shook the credibility of authority. Cold wars gave rise to suspicion. The oil boom dried up. Media costs rose. People became more independent. As marketers assured consumers that their products were good for them, consumers wondered otherwise.

The world demanded reliable products and services. So companies took the lead from the late 1960s and started to diversify into new areas. Yet, no sooner had a change taken place than holding companies started to wonder whether the investments would pay off.

The 1970s was also an era of short-term marketing tactics rather than longer-term stratagems. Many companies distributed their goods via intermediaries rather than direct sales forces. Profits relied on unit quantities rather than margins. Manufacturers concentrated on marketing their core strengths rather than diversify into product and service related areas.

The market no longer aimed at consumers as an overall group but at the diverse needs of individuals. So entered direct marketing leading ultimately to viral marketing. Thanks to developments in computing technology, it was possible to compile lists from clubs, geographic areas and surveys to pinpoint the right product for the right person. That information personalized mass mailings which, by addressing people by their names, enhanced an organization's image.

Marketing in action
When did marketing 'officially' first become a business tool?

Box clever (the Boston Matrix)

Another marketing milestone of the 1970s occurred in Boston, Massachusetts – the place that was to play a key role in later twentieth-century communications by becoming the first city in the world whose judiciary system announced a court ruling via the Internet rather than via hitherto normal publication. (This afforded a tremendous boost to the respectability of the Internet which, in turn, generated new electronic commerce – also known as virtual commerce.)

Again in the 1970s' era of 'medallion marketing man', The Boston Consulting Group devised an ingeniously simple way to classify products. It came up with a matrix of four boxes (the Boston Box). The Group suggested that every service or product could be categorized into one of the quadrants. The vertical axis indicated the growth of a market, whilst the horizontal indicated market share. Depending on the requirements and economic conditions, the given value of market growth could vary. Companies falling in the best performing part of the matrix had products with a high market growth and share. These were called STARS. Those with high market share but low growth were known as CASH COWS.

In cases of low market share but growing as a whole, there are PROBLEM CHILDREN (also known as WILDCATS or QUESTION MARKS).

Products which could manage only a low market share and growth were – and still are – called DOGS.

Comparable market share ——————→		
	STAR	PROBLEM CHILDREN (WILDCATS) (QUESTION MARKS)
	CASH COWS	DOGS

The Boston Matrix

According to the Boston Consulting Group, the fluidity of cash flow depended on the box in which a product or service fell. Then, as now, a common mistake was to confuse cash flow with profitability. In reality, profits help cash flow but if a business excessively spends in out-goings like Information Technology, machinery or even marketing, it could have what is called *negative cash flow*, whilst still making a profit. In other words, the money keeps on coming in whilst the expenses keep draining out.

Did you know?
Many furnishing companies offer up to five years' interest-free credit, with nothing to pay for the first year. This attracts would-be buyers into the market for furnishings as well as improving long-term cash flow and, as a fair percentage of the customers will want to change their furniture after five years, captures a potential new purchase before the customer shops around. (*See also* 'Cost of marketing', page 71).

Getting cornered

Virtually all companies have a little bit of every corner of the matrix. Most portfolios of brands cover various sections.

Starting at ground level, DOGS produce low (negative) cash flow. It's always best never to take DOGS at face value – their bite can be worst than their 'moo'. Let me explain: If a product (or service) falls between a DOG and CASH COW it is sometimes called a CASH DOG. These products roam the twilight zone of low market growth and share. Once a product hits the CASH COW box, it starts to emerge as a market leader, in mature or low-growth markets. The chunkier the market share the bigger the profits and because the market is relatively mature, you have to spend lots of money investing in production equipment.

If your product or service falls within this sector, you should think about giving it the marketing equivalent of a pint of fresh blood or a pep pill. In other words, re-energize the old by re-launching and looking at extending your portfolio. If you have a more modest enterprise and prefer a less daunting option, you should maintain your profit source by milking your product or service whilst grazing over profitable pastures.

PROBLEM CHILDREN are just that. On the positive side, products (or services) falling within this category are in a high-growth market. But remember, they have a relatively low market share. As with all children exploring their world of unlimited opportunities, the person holding the purse strings may suffer a severe drain on cash flow. To make the situation worst, PROBLEM CHILDREN, like teenagers into fads, instinctively hang around low-share product areas. So there's not much chance of making significantly high mass profits. (And the music isn't always that great either!)

Finally, you can reach for the STARS. If your product (or service) hits this sector, break out the champagne – but make sure you have enough cash to keep the bubbly flowing. This part of the box is equivalent to being a film star living in Beverly Hills. Sure, you are a market leader but everyone else wants to muscle in on your territory. That costs money – *big time*. You may need to invest in state-of-the-art machinery and you are going to need extra cash tucked up your sleeve to manoeuvre your marketing to 'fight off' any competitors.

Although the Boston Matrix is clever, you, as a business-led imaginative marketer, need to be smarter. So by all means refer to it but always remember, the final strategy is still yours.

Marketing in action
Your soap powder is a CASH DOG. List three courses of action.

Who fits where in the Boston Matrix?

Who	Profile	What you should do
STARS	First on the block. They lead – others copy. They are worth their weight in profits.	Pamper them. Maximize growth by giving total support and commitment.
CASH COWS	They've previously made their mark – everyone knows them – but can they continue to make an impact, considering that everyone has already bought their product or service?	Milk'em for all they've got! With the right management CASH COWS deliver the best profits. Keep an eye on costs – that includes long-term marketing campaigns. To revitalize your sales and maintain interest try sales promotions. Better still, add some extra service or product benefits by extending and so strengthening your line, and then create a bright new star. Ideal ways to achieve this include: • Adding product functionality to something – e.g. a vacuum cleaner with an added dirt-level indicator. • Evolving the format of an existing product or service – e.g. MM5 cameras into fully enabled MPEG cameras. • Adding a new way to deliver added value – e.g. from cash points to Internet banking. • Merging old technology with new – using toner cartridges from photocopier machines in fax laser printers.
PROBLEM CHILDREN	Growth looks good, for now, however, share is small. If they really are that new on the block, give them time to flourish.	Search deep in your pockets. They'll need your support to make it. That includes promoting them with advertising and/or PR.
DOGS	Real losers. Yesterday's wannabes – who never really made it in the first place.	You could try increasing your prices – might as well make a last-ditch effort to make some money or you could invest the time and money you would have put into a DOG into something more worthwhile (Harvest Strategy).

Product Life Cycles

According to William Shakespeare, man has seven ages. As we grow older, our outlook on life changes. What appears in one age as a gaping void, is bridged in another, through experience. Similarly, every gap created by taking a product off the shelf is soon filled by another. All products or services which come on to the market have a beginning, middle and, near but not necessarily final, end.

Take, for example, long-playing records (LPs). In the beginning, around 1894, gramophones were just a curious fad. In fact, the first commercial studio for gramophone recordings didn't open until 1897. Soon people started buying gramophones to play at home. That spurred demand for more LPs, so the record companies recruited more artists. Eventually, the single came out. Air play on the newly invented transistor radio generated consumer demand. That created a market for tracks – so the EP hit the record decks – a shorter version of the full LP record with fewer tracks, but more concentrated hits. This generated more sales for LPs which now had acquired a new lease of life as albums of a band's work rather than single snapshots. The entire process was a perfect example of a Product Life Cycle (PLC) showing a product entering the market, building sales, reaching a peak, declining – developing its stable of products – then letting each product (single, EP...) re-start the whole procedure. (According to industry sources, during 1997 UK record, CD and cassette sales were in excess of £1.8 billion. Today MP3s just about rule the music waves and tomorrow technology will go even further.

Today, especially in the world of technology, fashion and toys, a PLC may endure for only between six months and a year. The Internet has further reduced PLC through creating brands (so-called cyber-brands) virtually overnight.

Did you know?
The first UK Christmas hit record was more of a collection of records marketed by Messrs Perkins & Grotto in London. Costing two guineas, the collection featured tip-top tunes such as 'Twinkle Twinkle Little Star' and that spicy number 'Sing a Song of Sixpence'.

Typically, at the beginning of the PLC sales are quite poor. With focused imaginative marketing, people get to know about a company and so they purchase its products or services. Assuming all goes to plan, your marketing foresight builds up a head of steam and the product is a runaway success. However, steam evaporates. The product or service falls into decline and either you end up with a DOG or look at ways to rebuild, re-assess – rejuvenate or start again.

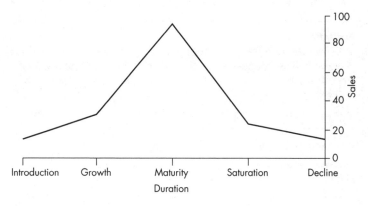

Product Life Cycle

Did you know?
If you are marketing a non-seasonal household service or product – like a diet plan or magazine subscription, it pays dividends to promote at the start of the year.

Sales teams like to refer to *customer diffusion* which categorizes consumers into:

- **Innovators** who will try out any new product.
- **Early adopters** opinion leaders who adopt new ideas early but cautiously.
- **Late majority** sceptical, buying once everyone else has done so.
- **Laggards** suspicious of change and buy only when it becomes the norm to do so.

Researchers often group consumers into life-cycle types. In the UK, a SAGACITY life-cycle grouping divides people by income and occupation.

SAGACITY life-cycle stages are:

- **Dependent** primarily under 24s, living at home or full-time students.
- **Pre-family** under 35s with their own home, but no children.
- **Family** main shoppers and chief income earners, under 65, with one of more children at home.
- **Late** embraces all adults whose children have left home or who are over 35 and childless.

Did you know?
The first UK company to adopt a distinctive brand name for a product line as opposed to generics, was Ricketts, Wills & Co. of Bristol which, in 1847, launched cut tobaccos called Best Birds' Eye and Bishop Blaze.

Marketing in action
You market a non-melting chocolate bar. Show how you will stimulate each market segment from innovators to laggards.

In Information Technology only the good die young

Lets revert to the story of records. Today, we have CDs and MP3s, as well as MiniDisc and DVD. No sooner a product or service hits the market than it is overtaken. The marketing term for this is *cannibalization*. That is, when a company sells a new product at the expense of an existing or similar one. An example of cannibalization which tends to annoy a lot of people is when a computer company brings out a PC and almost immediately replaces it with a new model that forces people to trade up. As long as the computer company's brand is constantly kept in the consumer's mind as representing innovation, the enterprise can go on cannibalizing models *ad infinitum*.

Sales figures can be deceptive. Just as you think that a rising STAR has turned to DOG meat, you spot a wag of the tail – a remote, yet distinctive sign of life. The reason may be that your product or service just needs that extra encouragement on your part to succeed. It depends how you manage your PLC.

Good PLC management boils down to getting to grips with certain elements of the entire concept. But it doesn't always work for every kind of product or service.

Reverting to getting to grips with issues – curves are not as straightforward as you may think. They take on many forms. Some are extended waves, whilst others are short and stubby. It's up to you to shape and craft each stage of your PLC curve, from introduction to decline and – yes, 'hallelujah' with a little imagination – resurrection. Furthermore, you should plan what you want to happen at each stage and how, as far as possible, you can capitalize on your achievements subsequently.

When is all is said and done, a PLC model guides you towards building an enduring product or service life. As with human biological life cycles, a solid grounding owes much to pre-planning or, in terms of products and services, careful research. In reality, nobody knows where life leads – but at least you can get your house in order to face each stage with confidence. Likewise, as your product or service enters the growth and maturity stage, thanks to focused planning and careful nurturing, your product or service life cycle can be long and prosperous.

Up close and personal (the PLC stages)

Let's look at each stage, step by step.

Introduction

You've got a great product or service – you know it, but the commercial world, more particularly your prospect, doesn't as yet. You've got to make a big splash. In addition to advertising the right pricing, you have to tempt the right type of people into your business (*see* 'Identifying needs', page 89). A special introductory price set quite low for a limited period would attract a wide audience. This is sometimes called a *penetration pricing strategy*. If you opt for this approach, gradually you can increase the price.

Alternatively, you could set your price really high. This reduces your overall marketplace but targets a discreet group of people willing to pay a premium for getting something others who are not at 'the top' of a market simply can't afford. This is called a *skimming price strategy*. (*See* 'Cost of marketing', page 71.)

This approach is often used by new technology companies when introducing new products for the home such as state-of-the-art hi-fi's. The great thing about this approach is you build up a strong core of top-of-the-market customers and later leverage for your gains through gradual price reductions to sell to the middle market aspiring to buy top-of-the-range products and services.

One point of warning concerning the *introduction* phase of the PLC – make sure you have the infrastructure in place to guarantee that your customers can actually get hold of your products or services. Poor distribution at the start spells disaster. It gives your competitor the opportunity to jump on the band wagon powered by all the hype you created. The competitor then offers customers an immediately available alternative.

Launching any product or service takes money. So, the first step is to invest only in something that can at least allow you to recoup your costs should the worst happen.

Up until the 1970s products or services had to build up gradually a market presence and eventual demand. Today, to make even the slightest enduring impression on a target market you have to pull out all the stops using imaginative advertising and promotions. Not only that but your promotions must be imaginatively designed in such a way that once you speedily recoup your expenses, you can move on to making real returns.

Growth

It's a big, bad, dangerous world out there. Your product is no longer as distinctive as when it first entered the market. That's good news for bigger companies who want to muscle in on your success. General statistics suggest that up to 60 per cent of companies fail within the first year of business.

Yet, it's not all doom and gloom. During the growth stage, you can expect profits as well as escalating sales. Because your customers know you, they are more likely to want to deal with you – which would be a good opportunity to sell them some complementary products or services from your portfolio. It's also a good time to talk to your dealers or distributors. You've proved your value. Now venture into other opportunities, like joint promotions, targeted viral marketing and advertising which create niche market demand.

Maturity/saturation

There comes a day when even your best sellers begin to get a little saggy around the seams. It's like looking at yourself in the mirror, entering that stage of life when the spirit is willing but the bags under the eyes make it known that you are too tired to do anything about it.

Look deeper, beyond the make-up and gloss, and you spot a downward trend. Profits slide. Prices fall as you try either to secure or defend your market position. When you are at the top, the ceiling of opportunity becomes finite. You are on your own, pitching price cuts against competitors. So what can you do to give yourself a little more breathing space?

Count the blessings in your favour. Your customer base is probably as wide as it can go. To maintain your market share, concentrate on encouraging your existing customers to remain loyal, rather than venture off into pastures green and untested.

Pareto

An Italian economist and political sociologist called Wilfredo Pareto (1848–1923) devised the 80:20 Pareto Rule – the law of the trivial many and the critical few. This 'rule' is based on the idea that, for the majority of business activities, 80 per cent of potential value can be achieved from just 20 per cent effort. Too many businesses end up using the remaining 80 per cent for relatively little return. This can be even less fruitful than it first appears. Imagine, for example, what would happen if a manufacturer produced goods which were only 80 per cent okay. Imaginative marketers simply cannot afford to look at the world in that way.

ABC method

A marketing method called the *ABC method*, classifies products into either fast-moving articles or articles that attract less of a demand. The Pareto Rule assumes that 20 per cent of your products – made up of fast and average moving articles – will take care of 80 per cent of your turnover. In my experience, the same is true of customers. Reward their loyalty and they will reward you – at the expense of your competitors. Equally, look after your distributors. If you allow them to slip away during your maturity/saturation stage of the PLC, you may lose them altogether. (This is one reason why so many companies at maturity level place so much emphasis on dealer and distributor promotions rather than just consumer promotions.)

Decline

When discussing PLC earlier, I mentioned that every product or service coming on to the market, has a beginning, middle and, perhaps, end – **at least in its first incarnation**. Consistent declining sales are warning bells that consumers are tiring of your product or service. Your market wants to move on – either geographically or tactically. Ultimately, like many businesses you could abandon ship as your titanic venture goes down. However, the end is not always as nigh as soothsayers would have you believe. So don't get out the hymn books to sing, 'Nearer my Lord to thee' – well, not just yet.

First, it may be worthwhile streamlining your existing portfolio of products or services. Second, you could consider concentrating on servicing a smaller market – as long is it is still cost effective. Third, you might still be able to put the brakes on a decline – even at a late hour. Ask yourself why, despite your strenuous efforts, your plans are going wrong. Don't be afraid to pick up the phone or meet your customers face to face. Ask them what you could do to improve. You'll be amazed how people are willing to help, especially when you are seeking their comments on your company. It's all a matter of adopting a considered approach before jumping to conclusions.

Yet, if at the end of the day, 'the horse refuses to go to water', it's time to move on. Go to the next furlong in life, learning from your previous PLC model and applying it for next time.

Asking the right PLC questions

Key questions to ask when your product or service has come to the end of a marketable life cycle include:

- From the outset, did you minimize your risks?
- Is it worth an extra effort to try again?
- Can you afford to invest that extra effort?
- Can you identify previous mistakes?
- Can those mistakes prevent future ones?

- Can you think beyond blaming failure on individuals and instead pinpoint where specifics went wrong within the overall marketing structure?
- Are you giving up because you can't invest any more money or have you lost your determination?
- Be honest. Are you just fed up with it all and want a new challenge?
- Are you mismanaging your team and so losing their loyalty to the firm?
- Are you brave enough to admit defeat and bold enough to restructure your plans?
- (Not a specific service or product issue.) Are you putting your health at risk for the benefit of profit?

Marketing in action
Detail a PLC for a Web TV set box.

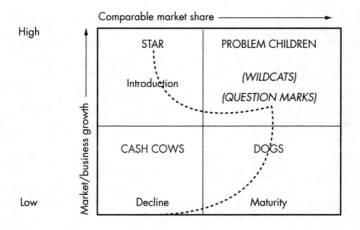

The Boston Matrix with PLC

The evolutionary Eighties

The customer is always right

The 1980s saw the merger between mass marketing and direct marketing. The sales process became 'through the line'. Companies regarded the economy as a through-the-line business, where product and profit control necessitated looking at the world from a global perspective rather than just a local commodity perspective. This may be one reason why, in 1987, Sony acquired CBS records and two years later Columbia Films. Sony owned the music, the technology and the outlets via computer games, records and films to control virtually the entire entertainment life cycle.

Marketing embraced the awareness attributes of television, press, posters and radio, along with the targeted benefits of direct marketing. It was no longer a case of 'pile 'em high and sell 'em cheap'. But, 'give 'em what they want, at the right price, spell their name correctly on a personalized direct mailing and they'll sure remember yours'.

From Boston boogie...

Meanwhile in the matrix-consulting business, the market was booming. Consultants popped up all over the place. They offered alternatives to the Boston Matrix. Moreover, marketers moaned about the effectiveness and relevance of the Boston Matrix. Some argued that it spent too much time caring about market share and growth instead of concentrating on the real marketing issues like gaining a specific competitive edge. Others said that just because a product or service fell within one particular box, it didn't always follow that cash flow would have to reflect that part of the matrix.

Other criticisms included the gripe that it wasn't good enough just harping on about market share being the 'acid test' for competitive strength – how about market size, or exploiting the strengths and weaknesses of the competitors, and how competitors react to price variations?

...to Boston massacre

Once word got around that the Boston Matrix was not as perfectly formed as it first appeared, criticism intensified.

> What if products are not self-funding? Come to think of it, who says that all STARS will become CASH COWS?

> What if my portfolio of products crossover or complement each other? Imagine I sold a three-star blend of Brandy and a five-star blend. My dealers want a company offering a little of everything. So if I were to drop one of my drinks from the portfolio, the entire range may take the fall.

Unquestionably, an alternative Boston Matrix was needed. The General Electric Company of America joined forces with McKinsey and Co. to create the General Electric Market Attractiveness – Competitive Position Model. Once marketers had overcome the problem of saying *'the General Electric Market Attractiveness – Competitive Position Model'*, without pausing for a breath, they liked how it worked (if not how it tripped off the tongue).

Instead of sticking to market share as a gauge of competitive strength, GEMACPM, along with other models, used elements, including:

- reputation
- distribution
- scope to improve cost benefits
- market share
- key points of difference.

Further market value-added criteria included:

- profits profitability
- competitive differences
- market size
- competitive benefits
- social, political and legal elements
- market growth rate.

Of course, marketers only used criteria relevant to their products or services. Often in models, each factor was 'weighted' by a number. The higher the number (or 'weight') the more important the criteria.

For example: (Weighted out of 1.0)

Competitive strength

Reputation	0.10
Distribution	0.20
Scope to improve cost benefits	0.15
Market share	0.20
Key points of difference	0.35

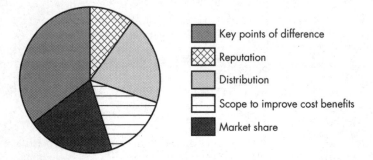

Key points of difference

Reputation

Distribution

Scope to improve cost benefits

Market share

Market attractiveness

Profits probability	0.25
Competitive power	0.35
Social, political and legal elements	0.05
Market size	0.20
Market growth rate	0.15

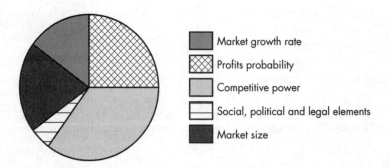

Market growth rate

Profits probability

Competitive power

Social, political and legal elements

Market size

Like a Ms Universe beauty pageant, each element was rated in terms of market attraction and competitive strength. Finally, every score (out of ten) was multiplied by the criteria weight. The results illustrated the product in terms of market engagement as well as evaluation.

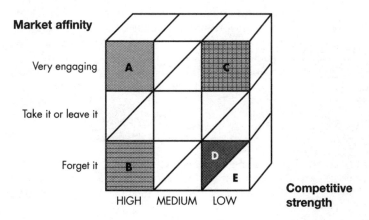

Note: Each area on the matrix is related to a strategic marketing objective.

The areas up close

A: BUILD

You are in the top position – a heavyweight champion (equivalent to STARS in the Boston Matrix). So box cleverly, directing your efforts into sales and develop your market share. Never forget that your competitors also have a powerful position, so keep your defences up.

B: HOLD

This is the equivalent to CASH COWS in the Boston Matrix. You should aim at maintaining your profits and market share. The market is not that buoyant but your competitors are ready to take on all contenders, so get your training gloves on.

C: BUILD/HOLD/HARVEST

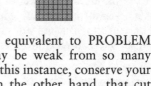

This is a bit of a 'tricky' area – equivalent to PROBLEM CHILDREN. Your competitors may be weak from so many bouts around the marketing ring. In this instance, conserve your energy, build up your strength. On the other hand, that cut across your competitors' left eye may be superficial and they may well have some hidden reserves to draw upon. This means holding your ground. If there isn't much long-term commitment to your product or service, you may even have to harvest.

D: HARVEST

Here you pack an almighty punch to protect your finances – the market attractiveness and your competitors' strength are at a low ebb. A quick, decisive, targeted jab could see them 'hitting' the floor.

E: STRIP-DOWN

Quick! Get in as much cash a soon as possible either by dropping some products or selling hard (the same as DOGS). Now is the time to swing your punches, left, right... *jab* before ending up punch drunk.

Marketing in action
Suggest two ways to handle a 'build' strategy. Which would be best for a high-street grocer who has lost sales to a cut-price superstore?

The informed Nineties and naughty 00s

Marketing ups and downs

The heavy spending on acquisitions during the 1980s led to bankruptcy by the early 1990s. Competition for business in the last decade of the twentieth century led to downsizing company structures whilst upsizing corporate expectations of employees.

Traditional job roles and prospects were turned upside down. Company hierarchy became 'flat' – with everyone assuming a greater share of responsibility. Unlike pets purchased at Christmas, jobs were no longer for life. Uncertainty of job security led to record levels of stress at work.

Managers had to learn to adapt to 'flatter' corporate hierarchies. Gone were the days of mushroom management when employees were generally kept in the dark and fed only tid-bits of information.

Instead of one company employing lots of people to do lots of tasks, specialist 'cottage' industries (people working individually or as family units from home or small offices) took over specific roles. This was the networked age of communications. It didn't matter where you worked, it was about how you worked and how disparate communities could be imaginatively linked. It also meant that individuals had to market themselves as sole traders.

Innovative corporations comply with marketing management modules like the highly respected BIT (Beacon Inverse Theory) paradigm. This demonstrates that flourishing companies encourage those at the top of a management league to become more accountable to people lower down the organization who rely on them to become successful.

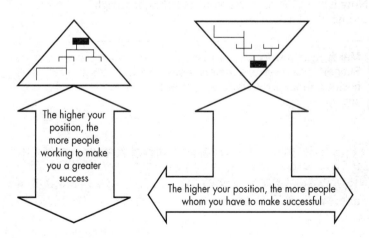

The higher your position, the more people working to make you a greater success

The higher your position, the more people whom you have to make successful

(Courtesy www.beaconit.com.au)

In the wider world, downsizing had seemingly smaller but corporately significant effects on business. Marketers from conglomerates increasingly delegated specific functions such as design, database management and sponsorship to expert companies – often confined to a few. The trend was to 'stick to what you know best – and do it better'. The original Saatchi and Saatchi advertising agency adopted the ideal not just to be big but bigger, not just bigger but better, not just better but the best.

Companies who wanted to succeed, invested and then extended their core marketing strengths into newer fields. If the Japanese could build something bigger or smaller, then the competition had to reciprocate, producing the same thing – but better, with more electronics and less bulk.

Marketing in action
What is the Pareto Rule?

Product Life Cycles shrunk. A new breed of specialist service industries was created. Its premise was based on a philosophy as old as the fourteenth century when the Italian politician Niccolo Machiavelli said, '*a prince does well to surround himself with serious advisors*'. With this in mind, stringent sole trader 'experts' competed against each other to win contracts for assignments. Small consultancies were growing worldwide. Some economists estimated an annual growth to be as much as 30 per cent. In the USA, a survey uncovered the fact that by the first decades of the 2000s around 90 per cent of direct marketing mailings which generated over a million dollars worth of business were written by independent copywriters or within marketing departments rather than by large multinational advertising agencies.

Overheads were further reduced thanks to breakthroughs in technology ranging from high-speed Third Generation (3G) links to international video conferencing and the World Wide Web. It no longer mattered from where you serviced a contract: the main criteria were – could you deliver – and *how soon*?

A poll by NOP asked 1,000 consumers to rank eight professions in order of trust. The findings were quite an eye opener.

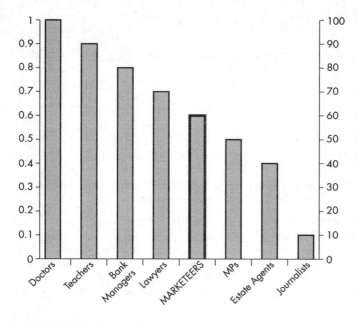

(Source: NOP)

Marketing in action

Discuss a marketing campaign including recommended marketing communication tools, which demonstrates the integrity of marketers.

The imaginative revolution

Irrespective of the size or type of your business, you possess the 'hottest' commercial asset – your mind. Your imaginative vision helps organizations move into areas which hitherto may have been thought unimaginable. With so many people chasing fewer and fewer jobs, employers certainly don't have a lack of manpower; what they need is *brain power*. Like a renowned football team will scour the world for talented players, so employers will search far and wide for talented marketers.

Did you know?

In the United States imaginative Internet code encryptors have to apply for an export licence to cover the knowledge contained in their brain if travelling to certain countries.

The changing face of the market

Flexibility in careers and a broad appreciation of the market have been highlighted during the first decades of the 2000s when crucial shifts in working patterns had even greater implications on core market structures. Just as the traditional male breadwinner could take work home, so women, traditionally home managers, sought and explored careers away from the household. This was partly because of greater demand on all 'workers' to be as productive as possible and partly due to the ever-increasing acceptance of women as part of an integrated workforce – especially within the management sector. During the 1990s, at last, success for women no longer crouched under low ceilings of opportunity.

Emancipation increased pressures on the family unit. Young parents had children to look after. It meant greater urgency to increase earnings just to afford child-minders – a flourishing cottage industry in its own right. In the case of British women aged 40 to 55, the majority would have worked for most of their lives by the start of the new millennium. So marketing messages would have to be adapted to match their more career-like views on life. (*See also* 'Sisters are doing it for themselves', page 102.)

Sharing roles as breadwinners, parents and partners extended to other important social changes requiring the attention of imaginative marketers; namely, the complex responsibilities of men and women. The technology had turned the home into the SOHO – Small Office Home Office. The advent of PDAs like Palm, meant that work would never be more than an arm's length away.

Imaginative marketers steered communications towards fulfilling a multi-levelled range of needs which superficially addressed one requirement yet essentially targeted a much deeper vision.

Perfume manufacturers marketed products which 20 years earlier would have been unthinkable. For example, men were encouraged to buy sensual deodorants, facial creams and soaps – hitherto the traditional domain of women. Taking the lead from jeans manufacturers of the 1980s, fashion houses were designing uni-sexually rather than targeting men and women separately. As 1990s European comic Eddie Izzard put it, '*all women are transvestites*' – highlighting the point that they were happy to wear trousers and jumpers and shirts from birth.

Just as the traditional work roles changed so, thanks to communications, travel and technology, markets became internationalized.

Did you know?
When Pepsi entered the Chinese market, its slogan 'come alive with the Pepsi generation' translated as 'Pepsi brings back your dead ancestors'. Likewise in 1920, Coca-Cola's brand name in Chinese was translated as 'Bite the wax tadpole'.

New millennium – old-aged, new market

A further development in the dying stages of the twentieth century occurred in the way companies marketed their products or services to the more mature market. In the 1970s and 1980s, marketers portrayed the elderly as the over sixties. By 2002, in America, marketers described this key market as aged 55 plus. (In 2003 alone, American citizens entered their fiftieth year at the rate of more than one every seven to eight seconds. Furthermore, by the start of the new millennium Americans aged 55 plus had twice the arbitrary income of people aged between 18 and 34.) To confuse marketing even further, this age group wanted the same goods and services sought by much younger consumers, for example cinema tickets, satellite dishes, snack foods and DIY materials for renovating – as opposed to building – their homes. (*See* Crinklies, page 103).

Small planet: Huge potential

Akio Morita – one-time Chairman of Sony, coined the phrase '*global localization*'. (The Japanese term for adjusting to regional markets is called *Dochakuka* – from a Japanese agricultural word for adjusting planting and harvesting for local soil conditions. The English variation is called *glocal*.) Today's community is networked globally. In the UK, new home builders feature broadband Internet access as a standard feature. Ideas, trends and traditions have become assimilated into a gigantic glut of data feeding the relentless appetite of the biggest industry of all – the service industry. Organizations instantly mix and match information from different countries as well as areas closer to home.

Such a pace is a creative marketer's fantasy and nightmare rolled into one. There is more than enough information to learn how to reach virtually any target audience and yet so much information is disseminated at high speed, that any marketing communication can easily become confused in a web of facts.

The bigger Mac

Globalization has a greater impact on markets. (Even discounting later financial disasters such as Enron, by 2000 out of 25 financial institutions occupying London's famous 'square mile' only six were owned by British companies.)

It is the instant gratification culture. The trouble is, with so much information to digest, it's often easier to opt for a quick bite at something familiar. For example, fast food companies like McDonald's feature environments which, in terms of substance and ambience, appear identical the world over.

Did you know?
When the Berlin Wall fell, top of the list of products to be imported by former East Germany was the 'All-American' McDonald's.

Imaginative marketers cater for the new tastes of a smaller planet with a bigger appetite for trustworthy brands. It is an approach which can pay dividends. Which is why, for example, in the UK during 1990, Mars changed the name of its Marathon chocolate bar to Snickers.

Marketing in action
Last six marketing problems associated with the NOW culture and recommended six solutions.

Market Eurovization

The circulation of 50 billion euro coins and 15 billion notes marked the introduction of the Euro as a single cash currency in the 12 countries of the Eurozone. Its launch on 1 January 2002 made it easier to market throughout Euro-land.

Whilst the introduction of the euro may have been a politically led decision, just as in every other aspect of marketing, its success or otherwise remains in the hands of the market itself.

Just as historic events led to a stronger Europe, so the Europe-wide integration of the new currency was years in the making. In 1957 The Treaty of Rome declared a common European market as a European objective with the aim of increasing economic prosperity and contributing to 'an ever closer union among the peoples of Europe'.

The Single European Act (1986) and the Treaty on European Union (1992) built on this, introducing Economic and Monetary Union (EMU) and laying the foundations for the single currency.

The third stage of EMU began on 1 January 1999, when the exchange rates of the participating currencies were irretrievably set. Euro area Member States began implementing a common monetary policy, the euro would be introduced as a legal currency and the 11 currencies of the participating Member States became subdivisions of the euro. Greece joined in January 2001, which meant that by the start of the euro's introduction the Member States of the European Union comprised:

- Austria
- Belgium
- Finland
- France
- Germany
- Greece
- Ireland
- Italy
- Luxembourg
- Portugal
- Spain
- The Netherlands.

Certain members of the European Union – Denmark, Sweden as well as the United Kingdom, at the time the fourth strongest economy in the world – didn't initially take an official part in the single currency, preferring to see if the biggest economic experiment in history would actually yield good results. This said, recognizing the new opportunity to be perceived as market leaders, many major retailers in those three countries quickly accepted both euros and local currency, especially companies operating businesses at airports and seaports or based in tourist areas. Almost overnight, business-to-business companies started trading in euros. Denmark's currency, the Danish krone, was linked to the euro, although the exchange rate was not fixed.

Do you speak Euro?

The need to understand basic marketplace motives – on a community by community basis – remain as important today as they were prior to the introduction of the euro.

For example, upon the euro's introduction, whilst hoping that it would offer an immediate economic boost, many Germans felt that all their efforts over the years to establish a relatively strong German Deutschmark would be wasted supporting countries with weaker economies such as Greece. On the other hand, from a practical viewpoint alone, the people of Belgium were delighted that for once they would have to carry only one currency in their pocket rather than a fistful of multitude denominations.

Then there was the matter of local tax changes, affecting the cost of goods across what was supposed to be a borderless Euro-land. At the time of the euro's full introduction, German value added tax stood at 16 per cent, whereas in The Netherlands it was 19 per cent and Belgium 21 per cent. So, for the first time ever, European consumers could see clearly at first glance how prices varied across borders. The euro's centralization of interest rates would help resolve issues but cause economic tensions and even higher unemployment in its wake.

Irrespective of other considerations, regional exchange rates also affected local prices. At the launch of the euro just less than two German Deutschmarks added up to one euro. In Spain a euro was worth 166 Pesetas. In Italy, a euro was worth 1,936 Italian Lira.

In France the cost of a cup of coffee crept up from six francs to 6.5 francs – as it translated into a nice round euro. Consumers became wary of marketing promises such as an advertised opportunity to buy goods at a bargain price of 'under 200 euros'.

The 'trick' for marketers was to encourage the 300 million citizens (equivalent to the entire population of the United States of America) who comprised the member States of the European Union to feel that companies were continuing to put value and quality before euros and cents. It also meant that marketers working in Euro-land had to instil a sense of pride in consumers and businesses alike for being part of an economy big enough to stand up to the American dollar as well as maintain self-respect as individual country-specific citizens who wanted to retain clear identities.

Businesses and suppliers working outside Euro-land also had to come to terms with dealing with one currency throughout several countries. Member States would have an economic competitive advantage to secure contracts. This generated greater competition which, as is the case with all competition, was ultimately beneficial to consumers and the companies that could afford to supply profitably the market's demand.

Today, whilst the feel good factor for Member State citizens like Germans visiting Ireland and paying in the same euro currency as at home is important, European marketers have to ensure that the new logo changes on currencies has greater positive impact on communities than the equivalent of a company updating its corporate letterhead, or merging with a competitor, only to leave a general sense of feeling that more has been lost than gained.

Marketers must remain vigilant that euro-wide brands continue to address countrywide aspirations. Which, in terms of the currency of conducting business, would have been a challenge to rise to, with or without the euro.

Today, you need to make marketing communication tools collaborate to achieve a greater impact on your target audience. The more informed you become about the process of imaginative marketing, the clearer it becomes that marketing addresses HUMAN NEEDS, PASSIONS and GOALS. These keys unlock the door leading to imaginative marketing for the twenty-first century. The successful marketer tailors every part of the marketing plan to be more focused on customers rather than the company. The imaginative marketer identifies needs and so offers products and services with the functionality to deliver answers. Such strategy-led marketing requires a blueprint. In the next part of this book we'll start to shape your marketing plan.

From 1990s selling ...   ... to year 2000 marketing

Then	Now
• Well-defined markets • Stick to what you know • Give the customers what they want • The corporation has lots of business • Push for a sale • Throw enough money at something and it will eventually work • Produce more and more products	• New opportunities • Extend your knowledge and skills • Show the customers what they could have • The enterprise has lots of strengths • Plan then sell • Invest less, but manage time to make what you have work harder and better • Offer greater and greater service

Did you know?

Six months prior to the introduction of the euro, a key industry report showed that, of 1,250 organizations across banking, insurance, healthcare, education and government sectors, one in three organizations didn't have a euro strategy. The total European bill for Information Technology to embrace the euro was estimated to exceed £606 million; more than 200,000 cash dispensers and just under 4 million vending machines throughout Europe needed adjusting.

02

shaping your marketing plan

In this chapter you will learn about:
- push and pull strategies
- positioning and mission statements
- dealing with competition
- problem solving

What made you buy this book? An impulse purchase? Was it the title? Are you what marketers call 'an influencer', like a training director who wants to develop new skills? Were you impressed that it is part of the internationally renowned *Teach Yourself* series – or simply because it seemed to cover most of the marketing topics you need in one easy-to-read bargain guide?

All these considerations – and more – are taken into account when designing a marketing plan. An effective marketing strategy balances and blends elements which generate compelling reasons to invest in a service – or in the case of this book – product.

More often than not, each component of a seamless marketing plan either directly or indirectly influences the other. It's like a giant Russian Doll. Alone each segment looks impressive – together they fit as a family.

Word of mouth	Viral marketing
Advertising	Sales
Sales promotions	Packaging
Direct marketing	Public relations
E-commerce	Events
	Corporate ID

Typical marketing/communications mix

Push and pull

I once saw a painting of a British army regiment fighting in the Boer War. (No, I am not that old!) What struck me was that, unlike in the movies, the enemy didn't attack neatly from the front; the regiment had to deal with ambushes from all sides. After all, war is never straightforward and needs orchestration to handle pushing and being pulled in all directions. Marketing plans orchestrate the relationship between a company and its customers. For example, if a local trader wants to encourage customers to come into the shop and 'pull' a product off the shelf, a *'pull'* marketing strategy is needed. Most pull strategies need some kind of advertising to attract a market, like pizza companies offering free deliveries – it could be a combination of television, press and local leaflets.

On the other hand if a company wants to drive a product or service into the mind and heart of the consumer, it could opt for pro-active telesales or direct marketing activities, in which case, a '*push*' strategy is required.

Pull and push incentives may include running prize draws or competitions, distributing special discount vouchers – such as pizza discounts – or even offering free software updates. When shove comes to push, push and pull often feed off each other. A company may use promotions to '*pull*' in a prospect. The prospect becomes a customer who needs to be professionally managed using techniques such as customer care services. Alternatively, stocks will need to be kept full. A full warehouse encourages or '*pushes*' a sales team to stir up business which, in turn, '*pulls*' the whole thing around again.

The power of price incentives should never be underestimated. At the height of the notorious British BSE scandal and the eventual Foot and Mouth crisis, supermarkets initially slashed the price of beef products. Despite all the scare mongering in the British press, consumers herded to buy beef. In one television interview a consumer was asked if she was concerned about contracting the fatal disease. She replied that she was, but just couldn't resist the price reductions.

Ultimately, effective imaginative marketing deals with give and take. More pertinently, it's about knowing when to do so and which tool to use, such as advertising, PR, direct marketing, electronic commerce (e-commerce/web-marketing), design and so on... That's why your marketing plan will feature an element of 'push' and 'pull' stratagems.

Preparing your plan

Before you get too involved with whether your organization is a pusher or a puller, you have to develop a plan to carry out your motives. Think of it like this. Like me, you have probably had to endure participating in meetings about meetings. Unlike a meeting about a meeting, the process of thinking about what you want your plan to achieve often *saves* time rather than *adds* to the bureaucratic process. From the start, your marketing plan must be logically constructed and so eminantly readable. After all, it's well and good producing reams and reams of facts and figures. But it's not very imaginative and certainly won't communicate in a clear, compelling way what you want people to know.

Marketing in action
You market a vegetarian beef substitute hamburger. Suggest two
ways to communicate your message using (a) mainly a PUSH
strategy, (b) mainly a PULL strategy.

Every plan has its blueprint

This is my business

What are your company's strengths and weaknesses? How
attractive are your products and services? Are they part of a
larger range? Do you specialize? If so, why and how do you
differ from competitors? Who would want to buy from your
company...?

My ambition

Where do you want to be in three months from now? How
about a year or two? What do you want your marketing to
accomplish? Do you want to increase your market share? Do
you want to extend your business through more outlets or do
you want to confine your activities in a concentrated area? How
does this fit in with your overall communication objectives?

Both (a) your business position, and (b) your company
ambitions have to take into account not just your expectations,
but those of your partners, shareholders, and so on.

Corporate objectives always take into consideration financial
issues like turnover, return on investment (ROI), machinery as
well as administrative costs. Often, marketers shy away from
such issues – after all they deal with the imaginative side of
business rather than accounts (unless you consider certain types
of accounting to be 'creative'). Knowing your financial
objectives helps you to calculate how to achieve corporate
expectations through the creation and on-going management of
brands, goods and services. This gives you the key to reach
financial objectives. Sophisticated Information Technology (IT)
financial forecasting programs can go some way towards
forecasting different business climates. However, no computer
program can fully take into account subtle influences on your
business, like re-training. Marketing objectives provide a route
towards turning corporate expectations into tangible results.

Communication objectives

Again, in terms of your communication objectives, what do you want to accomplish? Perhaps generate pre-launch awareness of a particular service, or secure your market position as being the leading choice of brand? Maybe you want to tell the market that your new orange juice has more oranges than any others. Eventually, all these requirements will form part of your marketing plan.

Quick! What's your position on this?

I once compiled a book called *The Meaning of Life* (see www.gabaynet.com). It featured answers to what must surely be the biggest question of all – What is the meaning of life? I received answers from some of the most famous people in the world including movie stars, royalty as well as ordinary people on the street. The best answers were the simplest. Equally, when it comes to positioning your company, a clear, direct, benefit-led argument is far better than trying to hide under a bushel of superlatives and thorny clichés.

So, imagine you have less than a minute to sell (position) your company to me.

- Who is your company aimed at?
- What, specifically do you do?
- How and why are you qualified to do it?
- Why do you do it better than anyone else?

Or to *really* get to the point:

    For   _____
    Only we can _____
    Because   _____

When it comes to selling yourself, you must be convincing rather than try to be clever. If you think writing a simple sales positioning platform, without a hint of ballyhoo or double-talk is easy – think again. You just might be in for one of life's little surprises. (*See also* 'Beacon sales principles', page 223.)

Mission statement

This should not be confused with either a sales positioning platform, corporate or marketing objectives. A mission statement is an inspirational executive summary which explains an organization's purpose and spells out its vision. Both aspects are essential when formulating a marketing plan, but neither can be implemented without first answering the second question of your sales positioning platform: 'Only we can...' – this forms the foundation for all your marketing exercises.

A mission statement clarifies rather than confuses your communication objectives. If ever an argument arises about whether or not an organization is on target to accomplish what it set out to achieve, the mission statement either confirms those key corporate philosophies, or otherwise.

Writing a mission statement, like all philosophical ventures, can leave you contemplating your navel rather than constructing a viable objective that will inspire your partners, staff, suppliers and customers. Good mission statements get to the point and avoid jargon or platitudes. They should be credible, attainable and logical. When writing, consider the impact of competition on your business and finances as well as legal, industrial, pharmaceutical (if applicable) and other commercial issues affecting future operations. Having said that, never write a mission statement as a predication. Essentially, the mission statement should address:

1 Why your organization is here (e.g. to make money, raise money for charity, inform, entertain... and so on).
2 The commercial advantages of your organization (e.g. 'offer peace of mind' rather than 'sell insurance'; 'provide the tools to succeed' rather than 'manufacture business software').
3 What makes your organization so special? (*See* USPs, page 143) (e.g. is the company better at publishing a particular type of book than its nearest rival? Does the mini-cab firm employ local people familiar with the local routes?).
4 Your ambition – every company must have an ambition; at the very least you should aim to achieve it.

One thing to bear in mind: mission statements can adapt to changing long-term circumstances. So if and when you have achieved all four points, it might be time to consider new missions and goals.

Mission statement hard and soft sides

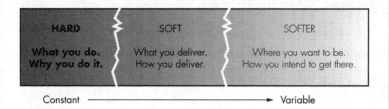

HARD	SOFT	SOFTER
What you do.	What you deliver.	Where you want to be.
Why you do it.	How you deliver.	How you intend to get there.

Constant ————————————————————→ Variable

Mission statement examples

The current mission statement of my company, Gabay

g Gabay is a strategy-led creative boutique. Our creative foundation is based on copywriting and related creative tools such as training, coaching and consultative advice, used as part of marketing communications between an organization and its publics. Through intelligent, accessible marketing, we strive to inspire and enlighten. Identifying aspirations we aim to deliver achievable yet aspirational results to clients, their target audiences, suppliers and ourselves.

We value innovation, independence and the courage never to make assumptions or ask 'why not?'

We aim to have fun.

We never compromise on quality, which is why we work with and alongside the most talented people and agencies in the community.

Our vision is to be the world's leading creative marketing boutique.

A Coca-Cola mission statement

We exist to create value for our share owners on a long-term basis by building a business that enhances the Coca-Cola company's trademarks. This also is our ultimate commitment.

As the world's largest beverage company, we refresh the world. We do this by developing superior soft drinks, both carbonated and non-carbonated, and profitable non-alcoholic beverage systems that create value for our Company, our bottling partners and our customers.

In creating value, we succeed or fail based on our ability to perform as stewards of several key assets:

1 Coca-Cola, the world's most powerful trademark, and other highly valuable trademarks.
2 The world's most effective and pervasive distribution system.
3 Satisfied customers, who make a good profit selling our products.
4 Our people, who are ultimately responsible for building this enterprise.
5 Our abundant resources, which must be intelligently allocated.
6 Our strong global leadership in the beverage industry in particular and in the business world in general.

Other mission statements
(Source: *Do you need a Mission Statement?*, Economist Publications, 1990)

Ford Motor Company

Ford Motor Company is a worldwide leader in automotive and automotive-related products and services as well as in newer industries such as aerospace, communications and financial services. Our mission is to improve continually our products and services to meet our customers' needs, allowing us to prosper as a business and to provide a reasonable return for our stockholders, the owners of our business.

Sainsbury

To discharge the responsibility as leaders in our trade by acting with complete integrity, by carrying out our work to the highest standards, and by contributing to the public good and to the quality of life in the community.

The Seven Principles of Matsushita

(Produces National Panasonic, Technics, National and Quasar)

- National service through industry
- Harmony and co-operation
- Courtesy and humility
- Fairness
- Struggle for betterment
- Adjustment and assimilation
- Gratitude

Brand strategies – less is more

Once you have considered your mission and vision, briefly summarize its essential message. This brand summary must be short, to the point, yet never diluted. For example, the former British prime minister, Margaret Thatcher famously said, *'the lady's not for turning'*. This captured the strength of her determination and the spirit of a political age simultaneously. The original UK lottery slogan, *'It could be you'* was the essence of why someone would want to participate in playing the lottery. *'Cool Britannia'* (accredited by British Prime Minister, Tony Blair to *Newsweek* magazine) was meant to capture the UK nation's dynamism. Pop songs, too, often feature short titles which encapsulate a spectrum of feelings, hopes and aspirations. Commercially, the longer your final brand strategy statement, the more time and money you'll need to explain it.

Marketing in action

Either rewrite your current company mission statement or design a personal mission statement as if in a CV. In both instances, note your rationale and consider your 'vision'. Then distil it into a brand strategy statement.

This is how I want to communicate my service

Which combination of communication tools (promotions) will you use? Advertising, PR, direct marketing, viral marketing … How long will you use each? Once you have decided upon your set of tools, you can begin to develop a plan.

I'll concentrate on these issues – the Six Ps (plus two)

What makes your service or product desirable?

Is your **Product** peerless? Perhaps you spent years in research?...
How does the **Price** match up to the competition? Is your **Place**
of trade important? For example, do your customers enjoy
meeting you at plush offices or do you want to highlight 'value
for money' by trading from a 'pile 'em high, sell em cheap'
warehouse? What about the way in which you tell the world
about your product or service, in other words, **Promote**
yourself? Maybe you use only direct mail or rely on
recommendations from satisfied customers. Are you making full
use of your **Physical presence**, such as in-store design or website
accessibility? Finally, what's special about the **People** associated
with your organization? Are your employees especially trained?
Do your customers have distinctive lifestyles or needs? Does
your team operate differently from your competitor's
employees? For example, do staff treat customers like friends
from the moment they meet (such as in an American-style
restaurant) or do they adopt a detached 'professional' kind of
approach? (One American technique concerning approaching
customers is to answer your phone, 'Hello this is (company
name), the answer is, 'yes' – now, how can we help you today?'
Perhaps a little 'cheesy' for European tastes ...)

Then there is what has become known as the 'seventh P' –
Process and its cousin, the 'eighth P', **Physical evidence**. Process
often refers to manufacturing processes including type of
packaging and production-line timings – both important,
especially when matching your deliverable goods to the market
needs. In the UK industry is service led rather than manufacturing based. However, even from a service stance, process
still plays an important marketing role.

The service sector communications mix

As I explained at the beginning of this book, marketing is driven
by the ultimate consumer. Your job is to win the hearts and
minds of your consumers. That means offering better value,
faster service, higher reliability, greater relevance and so total
satisfaction. To achieve this, you have to identify the kind of
environment which most naturally suits your target audience.
Environments may include economic, social, technological and
political. Every part of the marketing process aims at directing
the ultimate consumer to your company. To satisfy consumers'
needs you have to target your total communications mix.

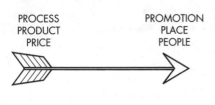

Imaginative marketing throws arrows at targets, not toppings on pizzas

Your communications mix may include a blend of any of the following:

- Advertising
- Direct marketing
- E-commerce
- Internal communications
- Exhibitions
- PR
- Tele-business
- Word of mouth
- Sales promotions
- Packaging

We do it for you

We:

- Develop a product or service;
- Plan our pricing strategy;
- Place and deliver our products professionally;
- Promote our products creatively.

Because you need:

- Something that suits your requirements;
- A keen cost;
- An easy way to access us;
- Understandable information to make the right choice.

The original marketing mix, named by Jerome McCarthy, was referred to as 'the Four Ps'. When analysing which part of the mix refers to your enterprise, you must always bear in mind that elements of the mix – like your company – can change and evolve as your company grows and prospers.

Give your ingredients a stir

Within the **Five Ps**, (**Four Ps** plus **People**) any company, service or manufacturing based, may have the following:

Product
- Guarantees
- Service support
- Quality
- Brand name
- Packaging
- Benefits

Price
- Credit terms
- Structure
- Discounts
- Payment terms
- Special deals

Place
- Types of distributors
- Geographic coverage
- Internet access
- Intranet options
- Store locations
- Office locations
- Transportation

Promotion
- Direct Mail
- Press advertising
- Direct response television
- General television
- Radio
- Posters (internal and external)
- Sales promotion
- E-commerce featuring push/pull channels (see page 209)
- Cinema advertising
- Product endorsements
- Test and trial campaigns
- CD-ROM and new media techniques

People

- Location
- Aptitude
- Industry knowledge
- Logic
- Team players
- Experience
- Personality
- Enthusiasm
- Professionalism
- Understanding
- Respect
- Care
- Vision
- Innovation
- Dynamism

Marketing in action
Using the above, list how the **Five Ps** are relevant to your business.

Sector mixing

Sector	Product	Place	Promotion	People
Service	• Presentation • Branding • Positioning • Reputation • Support • Portfolio • Performance • Lifestyle attraction • Quality	• Location • Speed of service • Accessibility (e.g. the web)	• Sales – personal and indirect (e.g. e-commerce (the web) • Advertising • Direct marketing • Sales promotion • PR • Sponsorship • Exhibitions • Design and ID • Customer advocacy	• Customers • Competitors • Employees
Production	• Packaging • Branding • Positioning • Repute • Service • Guarantees • Range • Features • Lifestyle attraction • Technical abilities • Quality • Performance	• Factory outlet • Retail • Channels • Transport • Delivery • Stock • Local, international offices	• Sales • E-commerce (the web) • Advertising • Direct marketing • Sales promotion • PR • Sponsorship • Exhibitions • Design and ID • Customer advocacy	• Customers • Competitors • Employees

---

Did you know?

Marketing timing is vital. It took 45 years after the invention of the tin can to invent the modern tin can opener!

Example of the changing mix

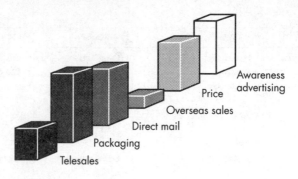

Trading – first year

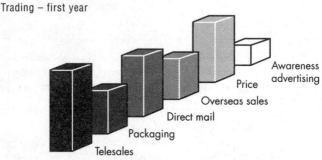

Year five

Depending on the development stage of a company, emphasis could be placed on awareness advertising or telemarketing. These are excellent for re-boosting sales or developing existing markets. Price, too, can be manipulated over the longer term through special discounts and limited offers to 'push' the market forward.

The DIY MOT (Marketing Overview Test)

With so many marketing questions all demanding answers, where do you start to find them? One way is to conduct an inspection of your company, or, to be more precise, two audits. One audit deals with the processes, products, services and people within your organization, the other with the marketplace and external influences.

INTERNAL FACTORS

People (e.g. Are they experienced? Can sales people reach customers?

Up to date...? Can your factory machinery cope...?)

Products – Are they viable?

Services – Can they be supported?

Financial data – Do profit margins look healthy?

Promotional data – What worked and at what cost?

EXTERNAL factors

Who wants you?

Where do your prospects go?

What's your competition like?

Can you match their offer?

Where does your product/ service fit in the PLC?

(e.g. Introduction, Growth, Decline)

What/who influences your potential buyers (e.g. social peers)?

Does government legislation open opportunities or prevent them?

You can liken the importance of carrying out internal and external audits to getting up in the morning. You get all wrapped up for a winter's day. Yet, when you step outside, it's a heat wave. Audits help to ensure that your clothes:

(a) fit;   (b) are in good condition;   (c) are appropriate for the business climate.

Marketing in action
Who devised the original marketing mix?

Samples of part of an internal promotional audit

Promotional analysis

Promotion	Where?	When?	Previous promotions?	Did previous promotion work?	What was the new offer?
Leaflet	Insert in *Auto Weekly*	Feb. 2002	Dealer posters	20 sales	10% off tyres
Cost?	**Target**		**Testing?**	**Followed up?**	**Result?**
£3,000 insert £1,000 design £1,750 print	Vehicle owners with cars over 4 years old		Yes – against offer in *Car Trader* mag. with 5% discount	Telesales	200 sales calls – 40 sales

Customer analysis

Client	Sector	Geog.area	Sales rep	Last purchase	Sale type (e.g. direct)	No. sales p.a.	Value	Cost to company
Iman	IT	Ireland	G.Isaacs	VDU Z5	Direct mail	30	£4,000 (25)	£100 per sale

Samples from external audit

Sector analysis

My sector	Current status	This time, last year	Key developments	My share of market	Hot issues
Rock guitars	Sector growing	In decline	Microchip for deeper sound, yet smaller guitars	5%	Multi-media integration

Competitive analysis

No. key competitors	No. cos. in market	Major competitor	Key competitor	Competitive offer promotional activity	What we did	How customers reacted
6	55	String Along	Ads in music press	£50 trade-in for old guitar	Match the offer	Still opted for String Along

Competition is like leaving a tea-bag in the cup. The longer you stand idle, the stronger it gets. Sometimes you match a competitor's offer and still customers prefer your competitor. It could be down to many external or internal factors, including style of promotional activity, service and brand perception.

That means asking more questions.

> **Marketing in action**
> Using the above example tables as a template, list a competitive, customer and sector analysis for your business.

Up periscope

A highly effective, graphical way of reviewing and reassessing the market compared to that of your competitors, is to imagine that you are the captain of a submarine. You are cruising at a depth of 1,400 metres (4,500 feet). Above you, a flotilla of ships sails. Each is a competitor. Before you decide which course to steer in search of new marketing opportunities, you have to plot your position in relation to the other ships.

Let's assume that you market luxury adult ice-cream called, 'Sinful Bites'. Now look at the radar below to gauge your position in the market.

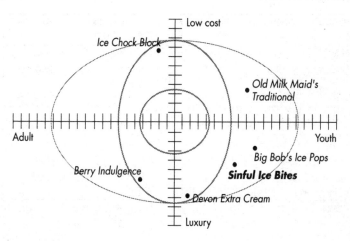

The illustration on the previous page shows that Sinful Ice Bites is 'hitting' the luxury side of the youth market. You may assume that it was in direct competition with Berry Indulgence or Devon Extra Cream. So this could be good or bad news, depending on how you look at it. It's bad news if you thought your ice-cream had more of an adult appeal, but it's great news when you see that your nearest youth competitor is Big Bob's Ice Pops – nothing to do with your more 'sinful' creative appeal.

Sharing the cake

Measuring market share can be deceptive. Let's say that during 2000 you sell 120,000 tubs of Sinful Ice Bites out of an overall market consumption of 1,000,000 tubs of ice-cream. So your share of the market is 12 per cent. Okay, so far, we are not talking 'rocket science' here. Now, another consideration: the weather takes a turn for the worse and summer is a wash-out. Total market consumption tumbles to 500,000 tubs. You sell only 30,000, so your market share is just 6 per cent. Should you be confident or wary about the immediate future?

First, you can never be sure of the weather (*See* 'Watching the detectives', in Chapter 4). Next you have to consider on what you are truly basing your market share. Units sold? Or money received? How about the share of ice-cream eaters (albeit sinful ones!)?

Getting the picture? There's more to this conundrum: How many of those ice-cream sinners were under 21 years old? (Statistically, ice-creams are more appealing to that age group). How many were male? (Statistically less likely.) How many female? What share of ice-creams were bought by married couples? (This is a proven growing market which stores ice cream in the fridge to enjoy whilst watching television.) What about those buying ice-creams more than once, twice or even five times a year?

potential customers ÷ demand = your market

The variables are endless. Yet if you ignore them by selling to every potential buyer who might purchase only one ice-cream, rather than market to fewer, yet more targeted people who'll buy lots of ice-creams, you'll end up short changed. You, therefore, have to concentrate your thoughts and energies into looking at more than one market share measurement. Do so and you can develop campaigns which don't just look good on paper but can't be licked.

Hoping for the best, preparing for the worst

Another classic way to identify your company's market position is the SWOT analysis:

Strengths   Weaknesses

Opportunities   Threats

S W O T

Strengths relate to either your company's or your competitor's enhanced value to a customer. For instance, a supermarket may offer shorter queues at its checkouts. Or a manufacturer may have a particularly good distribution system. So you can purchase a particular product virtually anywhere in the country.

Weaknesses could include a small marketing budget or an inefficient customer service department.

Opportunities could relate to watching for changes in consumer habits. Or competitors who have become 'uncreative' in their approach and offer.

Threats may arise from a competitor moving on to your territory.

You should carry out a SWOT analysis methodically. Consider *every* aspect of your business, including sales prospects, human resources, service issues, product availability, competitive positioning, and so on.

Unlike other kinds of marketing planning, like internal or external audits, the SWOT analysis should be kept short and to the point – in a bullet-point or table format. Give an outline rationale why a situation looks healthy or poses a problem. There are two compelling reasons for this:

1 It's a 'snapshot' of your position within the market.
2 Often the only overview key indicator, SWOT is vital in your final marketing plan.

Marketing in action
Visit three competing fashion websites and compile a SWOT analysis of each.

Keep tactics simple

When developing your marketing plan, assumptions play an essential role. They can include changes in legislation, corporate globalization, political instability, job losses and gains, project losses and gains, too many competitors – the range of assumptions is as wide as you can speculate. As with investment speculation, remember: what goes up, can also go down – so be aware and be market prepared.

Marketing objectives

Setting marketing objectives helps pin-point commercial goals. By listing objectives you can determine which of your products or services are appropriate for individual markets. You could sell an existing product or service to a new market or approach an existing market with a re-launched product.

Whatever your direction, you have to be sure of your objectives. If you are not, every other part of your marketing plan becomes 'woolly'.

You should be able to seal the **LID** on your objectives:

LIST exact measurements of your objectives (e.g. by costs, returns, share of market, weight, volume, etc.). Seek to **IMPLEMENT** a specific result (e.g. sell 40 per cent more size 6 shoes than you did this time last year). Set a **DEFINITE** deadline for seeing your objectives in action – Remember, *it's better to act first than react later*.

The Ansoff Matrix

MARKETS		
EXISTING PRODUCT IN EXISTING MARKET	NEW PRODUCT (*including technically improved*) IN EXISTING MARKET
EXISTING PRODUCT IN NEW MARKET (*or evolving market*)	NEW PRODUCT (*including technically improved*) IN NEW MARKET (*or evolving market*)

PRODUCTS

Born in 1918, Igor Ansoff was Professor of Strategic Management at the US International University in San Diego. He had a great reputation as a strategist and a bit of a marketing guru. The eminent professor devised his famous Ansoff Matrix in 1965. If a product or service falls within the top left-hand corner of the matrix, it is probably moving along quite nicely as the company has the experience of what works and what doesn't. At the other extreme, the bottom right-hand box in the matrix represents the biggest risk for a company. This can be one the most exciting areas for an imaginative marketer to work at. However, great results come only thorough preparation. Real 'creativity' can be achieved only once lessons have been learnt from developing all, or at least two of the other 'boxes'. Then, in theory, when it comes to venturing into *new markets with new products*, you can spring your service or product on a pleasantly surprised market without expecting any surprises – pleasant or otherwise.

There's a gaping hole in my bucket

You've probably heard of the term 'filling the gap in a market' or a similar one. Gap analysis generally refers to predicting opportunities for your business not covered by the competition. Using appropriate imaginative marketing, you can make contingency plans to bridge the gap.

The planning gap was another of Ansoff's brilliant concepts. He demonstrated the gap by considering the effect on sales if a company either did nothing about a marketing strategy or if a marketer developed a strategy to 'plug' the 'hole' in the market. Ansoff suggested that market share and demand for products or services from existing customers could be increased by adjusting the gap (called a market penetration strategy). This would mean giving existing customers more of what they want. Alternatively, a company could concentrate on selling products or services in new markets. This would generate new customers and enhance further sales (a market development strategy).

The more products or services you can offer customers, the wider your potential market. Choosing which direction to take – new products, new services or a combination of both, depends on the width and depth of your market gap. For example, if your chocolate ice-cream is bought by 90 per cent of ice-cream eaters in London, you could try to expand – and so close your market gap in other areas through market development by selling your ice-cream in other cities or diversifying into other flavours.

Below is a possible creative approach for a new line of adult ice-cream flavours.

> You went crazy for our Chocolate Crunch.
> You went mad for our Marshmallow Munchies.
> **Just wait till you nibble our Nuts!**

Customer buys	Customer hankers for	You offer
Ice-cream with nuts.	Ice-cream with syrup. assorted extras.	Ice-cream with
Lots of ice-cream locally.	Same quality ice-cream nationally. who also open up	Ice-cream to more distributors new markets.

Three ways to plug that gap:

- Improve your productivity.
- Increase your sales or share.
- Invest in different areas and resources.

Productivity improvements may include:

- making your sales team more cost-efficient
- streamlining your pricing (*see* page 71)
- making your factory workers more time-efficient, and so on.

Methods to increase sales or market share may include using promotions to encourage a particular product line or adapting your packaging to make a product more appealing to a certain type of market (e.g. the youth market.)

Investing in areas and resources may require you to expand in other countries or develop new products, both of which will require a re-allocation of your capital and perhaps even adaptation of your product or service to suit local tastes.

Before you start, consider the end – here's my strategy

Reaching your objectives is one thing – attaining them is another. That's where strategy counts for every imaginative marketer. Strategy is how to convey to a target audience the viability of your company, taking into account customer behavioural factors.

On your best behaviour

There are four sides to every box. However, when you are in a marketing corner you can never assume that every square peg fits into your box. You have to reflect on the dynamics which influence your customer:

- Cultural influence
- Personal influence
- Social influence
- Psychological influence

(The marketing term relating to the behaviour and customs practised by a society is Mores.)

Many organizations get so hung up about strategies that strategic thinking becomes a downward spiral wondering how to implement strategies. That is not to say that strategic thinking is a bad thing – especially for the imaginative marketer. What's important is the end result rather than the process in reaching it.

Marketing in action

You market luminous training shoes. Dividing your market into male and female, ages 12–18, 19–26 and 27–45, detail key influential aspects affecting each marketing plan.

Strategic Business Units

Some companies set up Strategic Business Units (SBUs). These independent 'think tanks' are meant to focus minds on long-term profits rather than short-term tactics. Multinational corporations such as food conglomerates typically have lots of SBUs. Each develops a market sector as if it were an independent company. All report back to a central board.

SBUs for a catering conglomerate may include:

- Fresh meats
- Beverages
- Health foods
- Dairy produce
- Frozen foods
- Home delivery via Internet

In Japan, rather than large teams of strategists, conglomerates rely on individuals who have an idiosyncratic approach to thinking. Such people look at customers, the company and competition as a whole and then formulate a set of objectives.

The leading Japanese management guru Kenichi Ohmae is often quoted to have said that Japanese strategic thinking is basically creative, intuitive and rational. According to Ohmae, great strategy is based on the Strategic Three Cs.

Ohmae's Strategic Three Cs

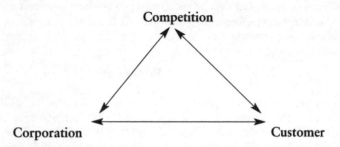

Each corner of the triangle has specific objectives and interests. A strategist must look at ways towards achieving outstanding performance *vis-à-vis* the competition.

Likewise, a strategy has to match the corporation's strengths with the needs of a clearly defined market. Only when this has been achieved can there be a lasting relationship with customers. Ohmae explains:

> In strategic thinking, first one seeks a clear understanding of the particular characteristic of each element of a situation and then makes the fullest possible use of human brain power to restructure the elements in the most advantageous way.

Did you know?
In the late 1940s, the Japanese travelled, picking up ideas for new technology. The best were adapted for local use. In post-war America, they spotted a system to get workers to collaborate on ideas for new products and services. The Japanese adopted the so-called Quality Circles System. Today, some 12 million Japanese workers belong to Quality Circles.

How would you prefer your strategy – with or without ice?

There are three main kinds of strategic approach. Depending on your objectives, you can adjust one on its own, or a combination of the three.

1 **Acquisition** of new customers. Strategies could include direct mail, advertising, e-commerce, sales promotion and cross

selling with other complementary companies (e.g. If you are a design agency, a print company could share customer data).

2 **Preservation** of your existing customer base and renewal of lapsed customers. Strategies could include loyalty programmes, offers to customers to 'come back'. On-going customer contact programmes like sending newsletters or viral marketing campaigns, regular customer care phone calls and personal sales visits.

3 **Up-grading** of your service or product. Strategies could include offering passengers a choice of DVDs during flights. Modern database technology is powerful enough to let the imaginative marketer recognize a passenger's preferred type of in-flight movie at the point-of-ticket sales. On the plane, the film is shown via a personal television monitor from a digital database. The result – an unsurpassed standard of customer care and so 'repeat' business opportunities.

Who do I want to do business with?

Where do your prospects live/work? What age group do they fall within? How do they make their purchasing decisions? What influences those decisions? Why would they buy from you rather than from your competitor? All these questions and more need to be considered. (*See* 'Watching the detectives' in Chapter 4 for further elaboration).

Who will help?

What staff do you need? Who will be responsible for what? Can your business be franchised? If so, what training plans will need to be made? Will you need to invest in suppliers like transportation companies, specialist manufacturers or inter-mediaries? Perhaps your business is seasonal requiring extra staff at peak periods? (This is discussed within the People aspect of the Five Ps – *see* page 52.)

What can I afford?

What financial resources will be available to effect your marketing? Does your product represent outstanding value for money? Do you want to make it expensive and so attract only a highly discrete market? How best to allocate your budget? What happens if you run out of money? (Please refer to 'Internal audit', page 55, and 'Cost of marketing' on page 71.)

It is vital to keep your finger on the purse strings of your campaign. From the outset, watch your costs. Seek a return on your investment (ROI). This is looked at in detail on page 74.

When should I start?

How long before you are satisfied with the intricate aspects of the business to be launched? Should you allow extra time for research? (*See* 'Watching the detectives' in Chapter 4). Should you launch your service or product in stages – testing its viability on smaller markets, before going nationwide or globally through e-commerce?

How I'll measure success

How will you judge the effectiveness of your marketing plan? Perhaps by increased sales or more specific enquiries? Should you put a timescale on your plan? (Many companies set targets for up to three years.)

Do you have some sort of system to assess productivity? Perhaps you set quarterly or annual targets. Maybe you prefer to maintain a dialogue with customers, typically asking, '*How are we doing?*' or '*Could we do more?*' or even '*Could we also be of service to a colleague?*'. (Never be afraid to ask what you may think is obvious. Sometimes by overlooking courtesy you may well miss opportunities). Maybe you can measure success by monitoring how fast rather than how many goods are sold. If you sell food, one method of measuring speed could be to look at 'swipe' figures from electronic point-of-sales machines in supermarkets.

If you are in the service industry, you could measure effectiveness through customer feedbacks such as questionnaires. If you are in the delivery business, you could look at efficiencies within your pick-up schedules. The ways to measure are as long or short as you need.

Collecting the information is only half way to measuring the effectiveness of your marketing plan. How do you make heads or tails of all that information? It needs to be methodically recorded, assessed and followed through. If you don't, the entire marketing plan exercise would be worthless.

Typical marketing measures

Profits

- Product profits
- Sales-team profits
- Franchise profits
- Regional profits
- Size-of-order profits
- Customer-type profits

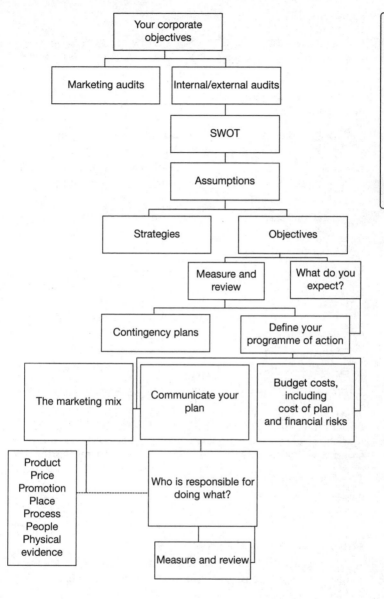

Implementing the marketing plan

Charges

- Expenses by customer type
- Costs by sales region
- Costs by market sector
- Costs by salesperson

Customer contentment

Tracking and dealing with complaints has become a powerful management tool.

- Number of praises
- Type of praise
- Level of praise
- Number of suggestions
- Type of suggestion
- Repeat purchases
- Brand perception
- Service perception
- Loyalty to the company
- Number of orders
- Number of lapsed customers
- Number of complaints
- Type of complaint
- Number of unique website visits

Instant marketing problem-solving frameworks

Albert Einstein said '*The formulation of a problem is often more essential than the solution*'. When looking at the logistics of the assembly production line (something he invented) Henry Ford turned the question '*How do we get the people to the work?*' on its head by asking '*How do we get the work to the people?*'

Likewise Edward Jenner 'cracked' making a vaccine for smallpox by going beyond the obvious question which everyone asked (Why do so many people have smallpox?) to Why are milkmaids less prone to contracting smallpox? Once you understand the fundamental principles behind devising marketing plans, you can easily adapt the formula to suit your specific needs.

The Crux and Nut procedure

This simple framework works well if you want a plan that can be easily updated as time goes by. It forces you to think ahead – and so, hopefully, stay ahead!

- This is the crux of the problem.
- Here are the different questions arising from the problem.
- Here are some possible solutions to those questions.
- Here is the over-riding solution.
- This is what is needed to make that solution work.

Marketing in action
You represent the UK Weather Watchers Organization. You are asked to formulate a marketing proposal to feature the sport as part of an on-going millennium celebration of great British pastimes. Use the Crux and Nut procedure to detail your proposition.

The following three-step framework is based on the thoughts of Helmhotz, a German philosopher.

1 Allow lots of preparation time to look at a problem from all angles.
2 Allow lots of time to let the problem incubate itself whilst you think about something else.
3 Open your mind to illuminating ideas which arise from the first two steps.

Psychologists term the inability to think laterally as functional fixedness or fixity. For example, the only purpose for having a saw is to cut, rather than to use it as a musical instrument. On the other hand, functional reasoning comes when you allow yourself to draw reasonable conclusions based on your knowledge of a subject as a whole.

Another creative marketing thinking framework to consider is the ten-point plan:

1 Accept that there is a need to make a plan. (You'd be amazed at how many marketers don't even get past this stage.)
2 Ask what marketing means to your organization and your customers.
3 Find out everything about a market from competitors to types of products and services – don't be afraid to ask questions.
4 Study the facts coolly and impartially.
5 Assess your findings.
6 Question whether your findings address both yours *and* your customers' needs.
7 Consider costs in implementing the plan.
8 Allow your thoughts to incubate.
9 Compare your ideas against your real business capabilities.
10 Get your plan on the road to achieve your objectives!

Making assumptions about your marketing goals isn't the same as hunches. Wondering what would happen if you did something is an entire world away from just saying you might do something without considering the consequences. So it is the same with building an imaginative framework to assess a marketing plan.

Thinking imaginatively about your options requires you to look at the evidence of your plan and then allow such evidence to plant seeds growing in different directions within a structured framework. Louis Pasteur summarized it as follows:

The greatest derangement of the mind is to believe in something because one wishes it to be so. Imagination is needed to give wings to thought at the beginning of experimental investigation into any given subject. When, however, the time has come to conclude, and to interpret the facts derived from observation, imagination must submit to the factual results of the experiments.

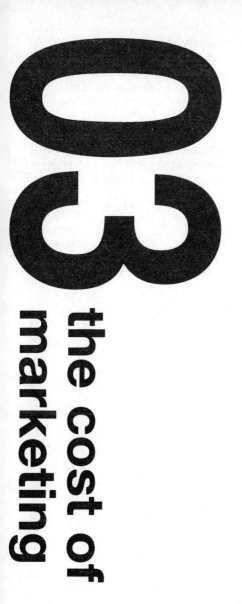

03 the cost of marketing

In this chapter you will learn about:
- measuring marketing effectiveness
- understanding pricing policies
- gaining higher returns on your marketing expenditure
- legal aspects of marketing

Economics is one subject which makes my eyes glaze over. As soon as newsreaders on television start to talk about the Yen going down or Sterling looking confident, my brain switches off – economics appears to be too much like hard work. This is bad news for me but wonderful news for accountants and economists who charge me vast sums of money to tell me that I am spending too much.

Imaginative marketers recognize that price and profit are at the heart of a well-planned marketing strategy. They complement each other like food complements health; without one being substantial the other can't survive. As such, it is essential that you have a basic grasp of how to make all those facts and figures add up.

John Wanamaker (1838–1922) and Lord Leverhulme are among the many distinguished people attributed to have said that *'half my money spent on advertising is wasted, but I don't know which half'*.

If *you* were a shareholder in a large organization and the chairperson knew the company was losing half of its money but couldn't tell *you* where or how, would *you* still feel confident in that organization?

I know an advertising agency which believes that every employee should wear the latest fashions and drive a limousine. One day, I asked the agency Chairman about his insistence on spending resources on chrome wheels and sharp jackets for the staff.

> When my people turn up for a client meeting, they should arrive feeling good, looking good and ready to address the client's needs. Plus prospective new business contacts like to deal with successful people who look affluent and act assuredly in the way they behave. I suppose clients assume a well-dressed person will diligently work to produce a crafted marketing solution. It goes down to that old belief that success will rub off on them. It's a marketing investment which pays real sales dividends.

Some accountants may question the cost of this exercise. Indeed, many like to see profits *now* rather than listen to marketing people's promises of dividends through making impressions *later*.

And perhaps arguably who can blame them?

Traditionally, accountants would suggest that the best way to set a price is to add up how much it costs to deliver a service or product. That calls for assessing the cost of labour, materials and so on. Then, add a reasonable gross profit margin.

It's never that easy.

Made-to-measure costs

Traditionally, direct marketing promises a highly quantifiable method of marketing. It offers tangible, measurable results from your marketing spend. However, even direct marketing can be costly.

According to what John Wanamaker and Lord Leverhulme said, general advertisers, who produce 'awareness' rather than 'response-led' advertising, can waste 50 per cent of their marketing budget. Direct marketers, on the other hand, claim a minimum of around 2.5 per cent response to a marketing campaign. (And they are proud of their response rate.) But even if in the unlikely event that every commercial advertisement performed equally and so that really is the case, it follows that direct marketing misspends an incredible 97.5 per cent of the budget – or does it? (*See* 'From junk mail to jump mail', page 200).

From private to general

Today, accountants tend to view marketers as tactical experts rather than shrewd strategists. From producing a radio commercial to printing a brochure, each task is viewed tactically. In doing so, an accountant may miss the larger strategic picture.

Similarly, when it comes to demonstrating marketing value, some marketers ask themselves how many reactive tasks – often generated by the sales department – are needed to satisfy short-term needs or capture a market share. These tasks may embrace direct mail campaigns, posters and so on.

Marketing departments are inclined to look at how much money they were allocated in the previous year, allow a percentage for inflation and then submit their costs for the following year. I once got a call from a client who wanted to spend the remainder of his marketing budget in the three weeks leading up to the end of the fiscal year to justify a bigger budget. To warrant costs, the budget is often broken down as follows:

We need £X
This is how much it's going to cost us to get to that figure. Here are the margins we'll make trying to get to that figure. We'll allocate that expenditure against prospects.
That gives £X for marketing expenditure
Finally we'll split the expenditure amongst different marketing options like direct mail, exhibitions and so on.

Financial directors need to calculate how much return the organization is receiving for its investment (return on investment – **ROI**). This often boils down to the general management belief that sales profits generate marketing costs, which is just one reason why, at budget planning times, marketers and financiers can be at such loggerheads. Depending on sales performance in the previous year, the X cost for marketing can either be sanctioned, increased or cut.

Assessing resources

Your accountant may ask 'How many sales and so how much bottom line profit, did the ads generate? What's our **ROR** (return on resources)?'

The key to dealing with accountants is staring at you. The answer is in the word *accountant*. Your accountant asks you to account for your marketing budget. Rather than make excuses, make yourself accountable. Ensure that your marketing plans make as much financial sense as creative acclaim.

Much of the trouble with assessing the cost of marketing is that you can't always base your pricing on overheads, like hardware or storage costs. In today's environment, the psychology of how you deliver your product or service and its perceived quality (the anticipated substance and character of your product or service) plays an increasingly important role. In fact, the perceived value of your brand has a direct effect on your financial performance. (*See also* 'Image is everything', page 146.) But how do you set a value on service? How much can you afford to invest in quality when you need to prioritize on more pressing needs like breaking even. What with the up-hill struggle of just fighting off the competition, who, you may wonder, cares about investing in extra whistles and flashing lights for your basic product or service?

What about building your reputation and brand? It all takes time, and time costs money. This is why you have to divide marketing budgets into distinctive areas.

Did you know?
Employees are one of your most valuable marketing investments. They are your internal customers. By offering the right combination of benefits from free tea, coffee and biscuits to a pension, even the choice of company car, you show you care about their welfare. More important than paying them money is to pay them attention. Above all, find time to listen to their ideas and so encourage them to feel part of a team. In return they become more pre-disposed to care about the success of your company.

Immediate business growth marketing

Here, the customer investment return is short term and variable. Providing the return continues to exceed your costs, you can continue to invest in growth.

Future brand growth marketing

The return from this activity is long term and sustained. Branding is accountable. It is much more than making your customers feel 'warm and cuddly' about your company. Without the brand, a company may be compared to a car without a body. It has no image or style. Just as you maintain your car so you need to invest in maintaining your brand. This reinforces your brand value and, like developing a successful car model, allows you to re-shape the brand shell to suit changing needs and trends. In this way a brand can be seen as a financial asset rather than a marketing eccentricity. (*See also* 'Brand marketing', page 149.)

The right time, place and cost

One way to value service is to price it by time. Simply divide your own time or that of your employees, into cost chunks per hour. Then calculate the time spent on a specific project.

Whether you arrive at a business meeting in a high-powered car or low-cost push-bike, leaving the right impression by offering value-added benefits, satisfying the needs of your customer is paramount. If the customer demands, you supply. The most valuable asset you can offer your customer must always be your or your team's talent.

Did you know?
For about £100 ($140), one ice-cream manufacturer imaginatively generated millions of pounds worth of advertising and publicity. He simply clothed cows grazing by the side of a motorway with billboards advertising his ice-cream. (An example of a viral marketing campaign – as drivers told drivers who spread the message as far as this page, and beyond.)

Budgeting for results – not resources

Accountants often view marketing budgets in terms of how much you want to spend. It makes far better sense to consider how much targeted communications effort needs to be invested to make a campaign successful. Once you accept that it's not what you do with your marketing resources but what your targeted communications do for you, you can budget in a brighter light.

At the end of the day, profits aren't generated by corporeal resources like machinery, brochures, direct mail, Internet sites and so on. Your definitive source of income is the customer and their expenditure on loyalty is measured in trustworthiness. The rest is just media. Therefore, before you can place a price on a marketing budget, reflect on the value of getting a customer. That needs answers to further pertinent questions:

• What are your existing customers worth?
• What is a new customer worth?
• What is a lapsed customer worth?
• Who are they?
• Based on the way they responded in the past, why (if applicable) are they currently acting differently?
• What have they been worth to you in the past?
• What might they be worth to you in the future – NET, after all costs have been provided for?
• Can you influence them?

- If so, how? Maybe a direct mail campaign, a poster campaign, a direct sales campaign, a telemarketing campaign...
- How will those activities influence how much customers spend with you?
- What's the likely overall return on your marketing resources?

More bucks for your bounce

Add all that up and you'll arrive at a marketing budget based on spending less time and money doing lateral tasks and better aimed money on more profitable areas. You'll no longer have to increase your budget periodically. You'll implement imaginative campaigns which make a bigger impact on bottom-line accounts for less marketing spend. Instantly, your marketing is less led by sales, less tactical – much more strategic.

Did you know?
Consider retail marketing budgets in terms of space. Instead of long-term rent agreements, utilize spaces along shopping mall central walkways. You'll make more per square shopping metre and so will the Mall's landlord.

Marketing in action
What is ROR?

Setting a price on someone's head

Everything about the Wild West is not as clear as it first appears. The famous Pony Express never used ponies – only horses. The Wild West period itself was a matter of years, not decades. When it came to placing a price on a convict's head, that too, was a hit-and-miss affair. Should a murderer be valued at $1,000? What about two murders? How about a kidnapper? $550 per person, adding another $100 for each ear sent as part of a ransom note?

There is a similar marketing dilemma in identifying how much to spend on either recruiting or maintaining a customer.

For a price, I'll tell you what I'm worth

Imagine you are a building contractor. A property developer wants to place an order that will bring your firm £50,000

($70,000) worth of business. How much of your budget should you invest to seal the deal? Would £1,000 ($1,400) be too little? How about 10 per cent of the deal? How about whatever it takes, even if it means making a loss in order to make a bigger profit next time?

Ideally, the more a customer invests, the more of your marketing budget you should reinvest in a customer. Adjust your expenditure according to the percentage you want to make on your money. So, to make the traditional advertising percentage of 17.5 per cent from your greatest possible source of income – your customer – you would spend £8,750 ($12,250).

Getting a cut of the action

The property developer has confidence in you, so gives you 80 per cent of a project. You have another customer who spends £100,000 ($140,000) on building per year but offers only 5 per cent of the work. Then you have three smaller customers. They offer the odd building job here and there. Each job is worth around £100 ($140). You get a project about once a year. What should you do – develop, maintain or give up their custom?

The answer is to return to the Pareto Rule (*see* page 23) – concentrate on developing the 20 per cent of customers who generate your greatest income. Then either dispose of the barely non-profitable smaller customers or gradually ease them out, promising that, providing they commit more of their work to your business, you'll offer an even better service than previously.

Alternatively, you may look at other ways to enhance customer value through offering complementary services or products. As a contractor you could offer site and building surveys. An accountant could offer EU tax consultation.

When dealing with customers who spend too little for too much of your time, balance your resources. If you continue to over-invest in trying to serve customers who only have the *potential* to grow, at the expense of those who are ready to flourish, you could end up cutting off your nose to spite your face. The same applies if you ignore the potential to develop other added-value areas which support your core strengths.

Identifying real potential from time-wasting customers again reminds me of the Pareto Rule. Which prospects share the same kind of values, needs and characteristics as your existing profitable customer base? If you don't have them but want to, invest in direct marketing – but I'll tell you more about that later.

> **Marketing in action**
> What is the traditional advertising commission percentage?

Balancing service and quality values

Today, with so many products and services vying for increasingly smaller slices of the action, to give you the edge over competitors, tangible quality and practical service must function harmoniously.

> **Marketing in action**
> What do direct marketers suggest as a minimum response rate?

You reap what you sow

Do you believe that if you pay more, more often than not you get a better service or product? This kind of psychology is recognized by the imaginative marketer. Price your product or service too cheaply and people may question its quality. Price it too high and people may not even give it a second glance. If you have a top-of-the-range product like a flashy sports car, a high price tag can be perceived as an added indication of luxury. When your product costs the same as your competitors' you have to add extra value through additional features or non-price points including packaging, service and quality. A typical example of this are Pizza producers. Many offer the same price, but not the same delivery times or special toppings.

Balancing your books

You can make more than originally planned. Set an hourly rate for your marketing expertise. This should be higher than the sum total of all your working hours, divided by your targeted income. By doing so, you can allow for discounting, negotiations as well as non-chargeable time.

If, for example, you expect to 'work' 1,600 hours a year (roughly 230 days @ 7 hours per day) and charge a total of £80,000 for that time, the simple sum is:

$$\frac{80,000}{1,600} = £50 \text{ per hour}$$

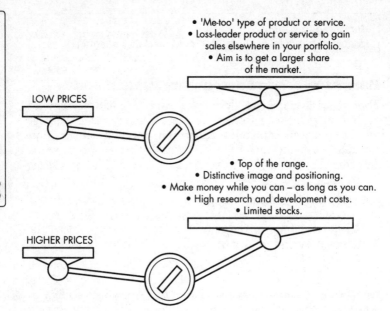

- 'Me-too' type of product or service.
- Loss-leader product or service to gain sales elsewhere in your portfolio.
- Aim is to get a larger share of the market.

LOW PRICES

- Top of the range.
- Distinctive image and positioning.
- Make money while you can – as long as you can.
- High research and development costs.
- Limited stocks.

HIGHER PRICES

To allow for discounting as well as any time that is not justifiably chargeable to the client, your 'official' charge-out rate will have to be considerably higher than your anticipated earnings of £50 per hour.

Depending on how much flexibility you can allow for, by charging just £11.50 more per hour – based on a general average rate of tax less any special concessions, you can anticipate an additional £23,000 for actually doing no more work than originally planned!

How much is too much?

Making money isn't just about setting high prices. As the late Lesley Crowther, a British television game-show host, used to say, *'It's all about getting the price right'*. Many retailers build global empires by offering low prices – at a profit – but selling lots of products *en masse*. Book publishers often sell relatively cheaply to produce short books for children at higher prices than more substantial adult titles. Part of the marketing strategy behind this could be because adults are happier to spend more on books for children, actively encouraged to read, than on books for themselves. For an imaginative marketer, it's all a matter of balancing production and demand costs against marketing potential.

Meeting challenges by managing demand

The 'demand slant' or 'demand curve', is a classic way of looking at price scaling. The steeper the slant, the less price-sensitive your market. So if you are in the position whereby you can charge more but sell less to people who are willing to pay a premium, the incline will appear quite vertical. This is a good strategy for businesses offering a niche service or product.

A typical example of this is a pop band whose fans are prepared at a concert to pay a premium for T-shirts and other merchandise promoting the band. Similarly, the government can continually raise taxes on cigarettes, cashing in on the addiction of smokers and their price insensitivity. Smokers will generally continue to buy until their last gasp.

The less price-sensitive your market, the more you can charge

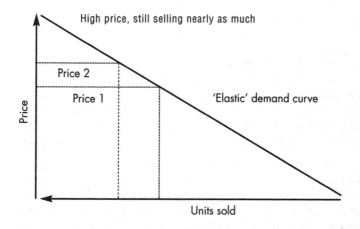

This is an ideal pricing policy for marketing within a highly competitive environment; for example, one toilet-paper manufacturer slightly lowering prices to gain sales from a competitor with an almost identical product. Likewise, this technique is profitably used by supermarkets selling own brand products similar to major brands.

The jump in cost for a price-sensitive product leads to a dramatic fall in sales volume

Drop prices, increase your sales

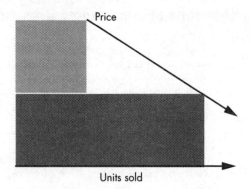

(If you can secure a firm brand loyalty, changes in price won't affect your sales volume. This ideal price plateau is called Price Haven).

Did you know?
Once you are a marketing millionaire, if you count all your money pound by pound, assuming it takes a second to count each pound or dollar, it would take 11 days, 13 hours, 46 minutes and 40 seconds to count all your cash – without stopping. Alternatively, you could invest about £400 ($560) in an electronic money counting machine and gain a good night's sleep.

If sales increase proportionately more than prices fall, then the demand slant or curve is said to be 'elastic'. (This is typified by my example of the supermarket food *versus* the brand leader's similar product). However, if your price is higher than the market demand, the curve or slant is less 'elastic'.

And, just because you might slash your prices in half, it doesn't always follow that demand doubles – or even moves at all. When this happens, demand becomes 'less elastic'. If this is the case, there's not really any point in using price incentives like discounts to induce the market. In fact, if you do you'll end up with a double whammy of lower numbers of sales and smaller profits. Whilst if your demand corresponds to your price change, the curve is known as being 'in unity'.

Like everything in marketing, demand slants or curves tend to be a little wavy at times. However, demand and pricing always even out at a point when supply and demand interact.

Discounts and channel distributors

Distributors are in business to make money and so will want a share of the profits. Those profits have to be shared across all the channels of distribution, (e.g. warehouse suppliers, wholesalers, retailers and so on).

It's all a question of 'live and let live'. If you want to get your product or service in front of the consumer, it is vital to keep the entire distribution channel happy. To achieve this, you can opt for carefully planned distributor incentives.

Distribution incentive	Benefit
Promotional cash discount	Distributors can enjoy cash cuts for quick settlement of bills. Also, a share of any specific product promotion.
Quantity discount	Buy more, save more.
Trade discount	Stock more, save more.

Did you know?
One classic discounting scheme actually makes you more money, the more you discount: invite customers to spend at least the same amount next time they call. Then discount any amount over and above the previous sale. They win. You win. Everyone's happy!

Another variation of discounting is Push Money or Spiffs. In this case, you offer salespeople added commission to sell accessories to your product. (For example, lens cleaning cloths to opticians, book sleeves to book shops, mobile phone cases to communication shops....)

When price planning an incentive, bear in mind that marketing costs can be seen in two different lights, namely: the profits you get back in the short-term return for creating incentives; what you can anticipate through developing messages in the long term.

Did you know?
Align your organization with a credit card affinity scheme. In addition to receiving a fee each time a card transaction is made and for each new cardholder who is recruited, you'll gain a new communication channel via leaflets enclosed with credit card statements. (Be wary of card points incentive schemes – with so many being offered, the market is in danger of becoming over-fragmented.)

What goes up goes down?

To discover the percentage increase in unit sales needed to earn the same gross profit when a price is cut, look in the column headed by your present gross profit and match it to the row that shows the intended price decrease.

For example, if your present gross margin is 30 per cent and you cut your selling price by 10 per cent, find the 10 per cent row in the left-hand column and follow across to the column headed 30 per cent. You find that you need to sell 50 per cent more units to earn the same gross profit as at the previous price.

	Curent profit margin				
% cut in price	20%	25%	30%	35%	40%
5%	33.3	25.0	20.0	16.7	14.3
7%	53.8	38.9	30.4	25.0	21.2
10%	100.0	66.7	50.0	40.0	33.3
12%	150.0	92.3	66.7	52.2	42.9
15%	300.0	150.0	100.0	75.0	60.0
17%	566.7	212.5	130.8	94.4	73.9
20%		400.0	200.0	133.3	100.0
25%			500.0	250.0	166.7

Robbing Peter to pay Paul

Customers view companies holistically rather than as specialist niche marketers who send out mail one day and then broadcast spectacular television commercials the next. So, it makes sense to go beyond evaluating individual promotions such as incentives or advertising campaigns. By all means get the individual parts of your marketing plan right, but always look towards the sum total of all the parts on your bottom-line profits. (See 'Gestalt Thinking' in my *Reinvent Yourself*, Momentum, 2002.)

Price planning

The classic demand curve requires an ideal world in which markets act in perfect textbook harmony.

- The demand is huge.
- Everyone sells the same kind of thing.
- Everyone is welcome to enter the market.
- Everyone charges the same.

The UK rail network used to be nationalized creating a monopoly. After 1997, the last all-British-Rail-owned train shunted out from a station. During the following year, the British railway system was split among a number of companies. If this had not been regulated, one company would have had total control of prices and profits. At one time in the United States, cartels of individual companies used to collaborate to achieve the same effect. Now in that continent as well as in Europe, such practice is heavily penalized.

In economies where only a few suppliers service the market, an **oligopoly** takes place. These suppliers may collude or independently set their market prices. Often, a limited number of suppliers go for high prices at their peril. For example, in the UK, prior to the opening of the Channel Tunnel, there already existed limited travel facilities for the British to travel across the channel. Prices were kept reasonably low. If one travel company – say a ferry company – raised its prices, the other enterprising companies would enter the market with 'slashed to the bone' deals. The same is true in the airline business. Although the industry is price controlled by some operators, once an airline raises its prices, in today's free-trade environment, a maverick airline can enter the market offering airline tickets at rock bottom prices. This line of thought is called **Contestable Markets Theory**.

On the other hand, **oligopsony** occurs when there are only a small number of buyers for a particular product or service. (The opposite, **polyopsony**, is when there are lots of buyers who want a specific product or service.)

So, price definitely plays an integral role in your marketing plan. As the demand curve or slant alters, so your plan alters. It's sensible to plan ahead to stay ahead. Returning to the Product Life Cycle, you have a number of pricing options available to you at each stage of the PLC. Each can be categorized either into a risky option or a less risky alternative.

Life Cycle stage

Introduction

The scenario:

Nobody really knows you. Few are innovators.

Take the risk	Take it easy
Whack on a hefty price tag. Innovators don't mind paying for something that's brand new – after all you need to recoup your investment. Or risk even lower initial profits by undercutting the competition and keeping your prices low until your products or services start paying for themselves and you penetrate deeper into the market (Penetration Policy).	Make an offer, try a low price introductory offer. Capture interest before charging high prices.

Growth

The scenario:

People appreciate your prices are reasonable. But watch out – the competitors are on your trail.

Take the risk	Take it easy
People are seduced by a low introductory offer. Subtly increase prices.	Keep your prices keen and your competitors at bay. Or go for a skimming policy in which your price decreases as costs become more manageable.

Maturity/saturation

The scenario:

Break out the champers! You've passed the winning post. People love your company. But just as drink can lead to drowsiness, so familiarity can breed contempt. Your customers might look elsewhere.

Take the risk	Take it easy
How long can this last? 'Milk' your product or service for everything it's got before it dies of natural causes.	Use your profits to develop other price–profit potentials in your portfolio. Offer even greater service to ardent fans of your company – but for a price which makes it worthwhile to you and provides that extra personal touch to the customer.

Decline

People are either complacent or fixed in their ways. Like a popular television soap character, you have become part of the furniture. Customers either take to you or leave for alternative enterprises.

Take a risk	Take it easy
Why bother with wasting any more money? Look to pastures new and invest elsewhere.	Keep your loyal customers happy. If they are going to leave they will, so you might as well maintain a high cost – as long as you keep up your commitment.

By the legal book

Apart from finance, another venturesome aspect of marketing is the law. Guy Facey is a senior partner at Amhurst Brown Colombotti, one of the UK's most respected legal firms, and has a special interest in marketing and advertising. He explained his overview on marketing and the law.

> The currency of imaginative marketing is genius. The currency of the best legal advice is caution. Combine the two. Your currency hedge should be some legal checks to minimize your risks.

There are many laws regulating advertising [in the United Kingdom]. They include trade descriptions, consumer credit and loan advertisements, food labelling, estate agents' descriptions, and more. Their enforcement depends on a variety of authorities – trading standards officers, the Office of Fair Trading, and others.

Your first port of call should probably be the British Codes of Advertising and Sales Promotion (the Codes). These are the rules promulgated by the advertising watchdog, the Advertising Standards Authority (ASA). If the ASA receives a complaint about an advertisement and they find that the advertisement breaks the Codes, they will ask the advertiser to withdraw it. If the advertiser refuses, the ASA can generate adverse publicity by making public criticism, deny access to media space (by asking the media to enforce their standard terms which require compliance with the Codes) and ask for sanctions by trade associations. Ultimately, the ASA can ask the Office of Fair Trading to apply for an injunction to prevent the advertisement. However, it rarely comes to that.

Apart from being prosecuted by one of the enforcement authorities, your advertisement could trigger a legal action by a third party for 'trade libel' if a piece of comparative advertising is so pejorative about the products or services of another person's company that the third party can sue for defamation. Compliance with the Codes would normally prevent such a risk because the Codes require comparative advertising to be fairly presented.

If in any doubt, speak to a lawyer first rather than have to face the costs of not doing so when it's too late.

Marketing in action

Which is true?

1 The steeper the demand slant, the less price-sensitive your market.
2 The steeper the slant, the more price-sensitive your market.
3 The steeper the slant, the more evenly price-sensitive your market.

04

identifying needs

Watching the detectives

The *Oxford Dictionary of Business* defines 'marketing research' as '*the systematic collection and analysis of data to resolve problems concerning marketing, undertaken to reduce the risk of inappropriate marketing activity*'. As you have learned by now, marketing concerns profitably keeping existing customers happy and, even more importantly, prospective customers. The links coupled to form the backbone which keeps people happy include:

- who they are
- how they want it
- where they want it
- which alternative they prefer
- knowing what they want
- why they want it
- when they want it
- how you can help.

Janet Jackson, the international pop star, sports a fetching tattoo which features a South African saying: '*Walk into your past to deal with your future*.' Similarly, the more you know about the background of your prospective target audience, the greater the benefits you can offer and the greater your own rewards.

In the twenty-first century, imaginative marketers understand more about customers than ever before. That includes everything from which side of the bed they rise, to naming their favourite evening drink.

Types of research application

Companies use research to acquire all kinds of information such as:

- customer contact
- competitive understanding
- new media testing
- e-sales
- direct marketing
- exhibitions
- advertising
- new product development
- new market exploration
- tele-selling
- direct sales
- events
- sponsorship
- PR.

Data intelligence

All information is a solid foundation upon which knowledge is built. Knowledge is the mortar which helps cement a concrete plan. However, information for information's sake is insufficient to target needs. You need to know how to interpret the data and by doing so, accrue intelligence.

Marketing intelligence lets you appreciate the brilliantly basic human needs which compel prospective customers either to accept or decline the opportunity to react to your imaginative marketing programme.

Ever since a gentleman called Ernest Dichter studied consumer behaviour in the 1940s to 1960s based on the views and the subconscious of individuals, marketers have developed the intriguing field of motivational research.

Perceptions

Consumers' perceptions, shaped by a marketing communication, is what psychologists call the cognitive cost. Based on how your product or service looks, costs or is delivered, people will react accordingly. For example, imagine you run a kebab shop. Potential customers passing by see through the window that your kebabs are dripping congealed lumps of fat. From a PR viewpoint, cognitive cost may be too high to digest. Similarly, if you sell DIY furniture and the instructions appear too complicated, even before reading a word, the confused DIYer would assume that the process is too convoluted.

From the outset, your product or service must appeal to a prospective buyer's psychological needs. In 1970, one of the twentieth century's greatest psychologists died. Abraham Maslow left a legacy which included one of today's most often quoted target market research formulas – Maslow's pyramid.

Maslow argued that there are five sets of motivational factors which influence people. As each need intensifies it evolves into a motive to be fulfilled. Your job is to fuel that need so the person acts or is influenced by your marketing message. Once that motive is satisfied, a person steps up to the next level in the pyramid. Compelling motives further escalate towards the pyramid's pinnacle. Imaginative marketers aim to ensure that, through understanding how to balance complex personal emotions with goals, the pyramid's hierarchy is easily fulfilled.

At one time pensions and life assurance were some of the most significant growth areas within the UK marketing sector. In 1995, the world's population stood at 5.7 billion (UK). By 2050, the world's population could swell to a staggering 10 billion (UK). During the twenty-first century, people's perceptions of

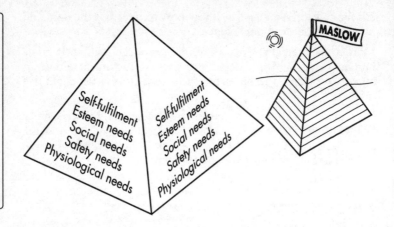

the state caring for their future welfare will be most probably as eroded as actual state benefits. According to a report which I heard on Talk Radio in Oregon, pills were offered to terminally ill patients with only about six months to live. The pills would end the patients' lives as well as ending the welfare burden to the local health sector.

Right now, imaginative marketers are in a powerful position to influence would-be pensioners to buy private pensions and health plans. Looking at the Maslow model, you could adapt your communication messages as follows:

1 **Physiological needs**
   Will a pension pay for food and shelter?

2 **Safety needs**
   Will a pension protect the family's welfare?

3 **Social needs**
   Will a pension enable continued membership of a sports or social club?

4 **Esteem needs**
   Will a pension maintain a lifestyle?

5 **Self-fulfilment needs**
   Will a pension free a customer to achieve later what the customer is too busy to achieve currently?

Pension power will also affect other industries such as fashion retailing. By 2003, people aged 62 plus will account for around

20 per cent of the retail fashion sector. Every seven years, the sector redefines 'old' by adding another two years to its previous age limit.

Marketing in action
What do you think are your customers' cognitive costs?

Freudian Theory of Motivation

Sigmund Freud (1856–1939), the renowned psychologist, held an opposing view to that of Maslow. He argued that from a psychosocial view, people didn't consciously realize what motivated them. Instead of systematically addressing needs, Freud suggested, people repressed cravings only to deal with them through dreams, slips of the tongue (Freudian slips) neurotically, phobically, obsessively or psychotically. So, from Freud's perspective, someone who hankers to give up smoking may suck on a plastic cigarette which reminds him/her of suckling at a mother's breasts.

A woman in a television commercial standing beneath a waterfall with her mouth open to the freshness of the stream, overtly representing the 'fresh' taste of a mint, may in fact covertly represent something far more libidinous.

A woman may use a strong detergent to clean her kitchen because, as in Shakespeare's Lady Macbeth character who vainly tries to clean her hands of her crime, she feels 'dirty' about guilt within herself.

> Out, damnéd spot! out, I say! One: two: why, then 'tis time to do't. Hell is murky!
>
> (*Macbeth*, Act V, scene 1)

Arguably – although stretching it a bit! – a man at work may want to write with an expensive, chunky pen because he feels sexually inadequate. A woman may enjoy an ice-lolly because it is phallic. (Great news for marketers working on the Sinful Ice Bites project! – *See* 'Sharing the cake', page 58.) Teenagers may surf the World Wide Web in search of Blog sites, because deep down they want to break free from the confines of their parental home. On the other hand, they may just want to have a bit of fun – *What do you think?*

Market research techniques seeking personal interpretations learnt from one-to-one interviews, adopt a psychoanalytical approach to pin-pointed motives. This method often spawns Freudian interpretations. On the other hand, a psychological approach towards motivational research asks groups to relate their collective feelings, influenced by their social culture and environment.

Did you know?
Enterprising imaginative marketers have helped turn the understanding of human motives into a huge industry. It is estimated that in the United States, there are over 415 types of therapy available; from cognitive behaviour therapy to existential psychotherapy. Best of all, many sessions can be 'charged' to heavily marketed private health schemes!

Power is the greatest aphrodisiac of all (Henry Kissinger)

It is interesting to ponder on how much research into personal drives and motives actually has a serious relevance on a person's public and professional life. For instance, can an individual's clandestine obsessions have any adverse effect on his/her persona grata status – and so relevance to a common market? Are that person's public and personal thoughts interrelated – even if subconsciously? If so, are these important factors to consider when trying to understand hidden motives to either accept or reject a marketing proposition?

Two years before the planned completion of his second term presidency, the world gasped when it was alleged that US President Clinton had possibly had affairs with several women. Worse still, they were supposed to have occurred within the precincts of the White House. Prior to previous and similar accusations initially being thrown out of court, later to be accepted, in addition to his own initial denial, the President's wife contested that it was part of a political right-wing conspiracy. Political as well as social commentators around the world questioned whether a man in his fifties, apparently unable to control his sexual urges was suitable to control the nuclear arms of the most powerful nation on earth. On the other hand, should someone with a tight grasp on foreign affairs be criticized because he had a looser hold on personal ones?

Some argue that, given half a chance, men, by their nature, even in the third millennium New Sexual Age, would naturally have an extra-marital sexual affair. Indeed, in some European countries and Middle and Far Eastern countries it would be considered odd if a male leader in power never strayed. (Historically, the Emperor of Japan would regularly be supplied with concubines on the premise that a personally fulfilled Emperor would make better policy decisions.)

Assessing personal motives – especially provocative ones – is why all research questions must be asked in context. If not, wrong conclusions can be drawn about the propensity of a target audience towards something, which may in reality, have little or no bearing on a wider, more relevant issue.

Did you know?
Unlike the Americans, spouses of some British men have less to worry about concerning infidelity. A widely reported survey revealed that 95 per cent of men aged 20 to 34 would prefer to watch football on television than have sex with a supermodel.

Thinking deeper

Ever since experiments took place in California during the late 1960s and early 1970s, neurologists believe each side of the human brain specializes in certain regions of consciousness housed within a pleated casing, some 2.5 mm (0.1 inches) thick, called the cerebral cortex.

Each of the two hemispheres has lots of cavities called ventricles. Prior to modern scientific understanding, people thought that these ventricles cupped the human spirit. Both hemispheres are connected by an intricate collection of nerve fibres called the Corpus Callosum. The left side of the brain deals with practical issues and controls the right side of the body. The right side of the brain deals with creative and symbolic issues as well as controlling the left side of the body. Marketing researchers developed this into an area called braintyping.

Strategic marketers have often cited that a typical 'left-brain' thinking person is thought good at understanding order and structure. (This side is particularly apt at language skills). Ideally, at our most imaginative, we make best use of both spheres.

Did you know?
Even taking your marketing brilliance into account, the difference between your DNA and that of a chimpanzee is less than 1 per cent.

The typical 'right-brain' thinking person is meant to be creative and emotionally led. Some business consultants believe that certain business managers don't exercise enough mentally. They may worry too much about tactics rather than allow themselves freedom of self-expression. The extent of the problem is such that the manager becomes stressed. Marketers, as well as neurologists, further assert that most people are influenced by one side or the other. Yet, unless mentally impeded, nobody thinks just linearly with either! So people don't look at marketing campaigns wearing either just their 'creative' or 'logical' thinking cap.

The imaginative marketer connects right and left brain potential.

Tactical, disconnected thinking can lead to 'half-baked' ideas.

Through visualizing an ambition and detailing a supporting plan you can aim for an achievable marketing goal.

Inspiration in a flash

Each side of the brain comprises subsystems of some 10,000 million brain cells (or neurons). Neurons allow messages – including marketing messages – to enter and leave the brain and the nervous system, once your marketing communication has been 'registered' by your customer, a dendrite which is like a star burst at the end of the neuron, converts it into an electric signal transmitted all the way down through the nervous system.

Because both right and left sectors of the brain are capable, to a degree, of thinking both laterally as well as lucidly, based on the way you present your company, a consumer may or may not act on a hunch to buy. So as you can see, it's all about getting the marketing communications chemistry right – in more senses than one.

Did you know?
Although it has become a visual cliché, the imaginative marketer really can light up a bulb with every new idea: the brain runs at a power rating of 10 watts per minute and radiates 20 per cent of body heat.

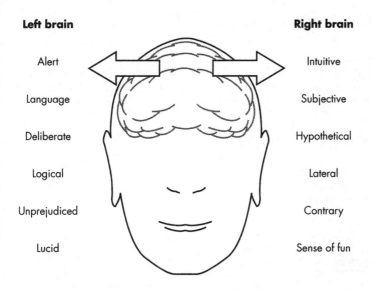

Left brain

Alert

Language

Deliberate

Logical

Unprejudiced

Lucid

Right brain

Intuitive

Subjective

Hypothetical

Lateral

Contrary

Sense of fun

Don't ask 'why?' Question 'why not?'

Before you can discover why people may want to deal with you, cast a net wider across the pyschographic as well as demographic nature of your prospective audience. Traditionally, marketers categorized their audience in terms of social standing. This is particularly true in the United Kingdom where the entire social structure is based on pecking order in terms of power, money and heritage.

Socio-economic grouping or 'social grading' was first developed by the Institute of Practitioners in Advertising. The system classifies social status according to interests, social background and occupation. Each piece of data reflects the job of the head of the household. In the past, however, socio-economic classification tended to grade people by their income.

Social grade	Social status	Occupation of the head of household
A	Upper middle class	Higher managerial Professional
B	Middle class managerial	Intermediate
C1	Lower middle class	Clerical
C2	Skilled working class	Skilled manual worker
D	Working class	Unskilled manual worker
E	Lowest level	State pensioner widow, casual worker, people dependent on social security

(Source: JICNARS national readership survey)

In the United States, there is no such universal system to grade people by social status. Instead, American marketers rely on lifestyle data and neighbourhood or geodemographics data such as those often used in UK direct marketing. (*See also* 'VALS', page 100.)

European values in a TEA cup

European classification is harder to pinpoint. However, the European Society for Opinion and Marketing Research (ESOMAR) has gone a long way to harmonize social-grade classifications. Their marketing classification index covers: Austria, Belgium, Denmark, Finland, France, Germany, Greece, Ireland, Italy, Luxembourg, the Netherlands, Portugal, Spain, Sweden and the United Kingdom.

ESOMAR grades are based on Terminal Education Age (TEA) as well as the job and the primary household income earner. If the main income earner is unemployed, his/her occupation is replaced by the general economic status of the household. This is based on ownership of ten consumer durables:

- second home or holiday home/flat
- two or more cars
- personal computer/ home computer
- colour television
- video camera
- video/DVD recorder
- still camera
- electric drill
- electric deep-fat fryer
- clock radio.

The items may be replaced where appropriate in certain countries. In theory, the more items owned, the higher the socio grade.

Each country has a different TEA, so you can appreciate that occasionally it may difficult to provide a universal grading example. However, a socially categorized E(1) may include skilled workers with a TEA of 17–18. (In Portugal, the TEA is much lower as children leave school at 14.)

Marketing in action
True or false? A left-brain thinker is good at understanding creative issues.

Social category	Description
AB	Managers and professionals
C1	Well-educated non-manual employees
C2	Skilled workers and non-manual employees
DE	Unskilled manual workers and other less educated workers/employees

(Source: ESOMAR)

Psychographic targeting models

Have you noticed those stickers at the back of cars – SURFERS DO IT STANDING UP or MARKETING REPS DO IT ON COMMISSION, MATCH-MAKERS DO IT WITH SINGLES, ADVERTISERS USE THE NEW IMPROVED METHOD, DIRECT MARKETERS DO IT WITH A MONEY BACK GUARANTEE...? Well, imaginative marketers have many lifestyle oriented methods of classifying people at their disposal.

Psychographic or psychometric classification targets consumers by attitudes and other intellectual characteristics such as hobbies, interests, political views, family values and career goals, has led to various acronyms and classifications of typical consumers. This kind of classification has been adapted by many market research companies to match specific market-testing needs. Typically, such adaptations have included matching intellectual characteristics against age, sex, shopping types, management types, car owner types ... the list is endless.

For example, you could categorize consumers by movie-star fans:

Type	Possible characteristic
J-Lo – Babe	Experimental, owner-occupier, Webucated
Sharon Stone – Believer	House proud, sharing, middle class
Vinne Jones – Doer	Working class, lower income, social realist
Susan Sarandon – Mover	Affluent, interested in cultural issues, sophisticated
Keanu Reeves – Non-conformist	Sociable, moralist (acting on personal agenda)

Did you know?
A common method to classify a product or service is to liken it to a food or colour. It helps to identify social attributes and character. (*See also* 'TAT' in 'Jargon busters', page 235.)

Another way to 'name-tag' groups of people into marketing consumer types is the Values and Lifestyles approach (VALS™). This classification, originally devised in 1978 by Arnold Mitchell of SRI International (formerly Standford Research Institute), tracks people as they progress from being altogether apathetic to socially perceptive and virtuously vivacious.

Survivors	Extremely poor and despondent
Sustainers future	Poor, but slightly optimistic about the
Belongers	Conventional, middle-of-the-road types who like to fit in
Emulators conscious	Aspiring, upwardly mobile and status
Achievers	Successful leaders
I-am-me's	Young, self-aware and self-driven; usually acting on the spur of the moment
Experimentals egocentric	Hedonists keen to experiment, yet
Society conscious injustice	Strive to wipe out examples of all social
Mature integrated	Socially balanced, inwardly confident

(Based on the original Value-Added Lifestyles typology)

VALS™ 2 Lifestyles program segments American consumers and so helps imaginative marketers predict behaviour.

According to information provided by SRI International, consumers are driven by one of three powerful self-orientations: **principle**, **status** and **action**.

Principle-orientated consumers are guided in their choices by abstract, idealized criteria as opposed to feelings, events or desire for approval and opinions of others.

Status-orientated consumers seek products and services that demonstrate the consumers' success to their peers.

Action-type consumers are driven by a desire for social or physical activity, variety and risk taking.

Within the VALS™ 2 system there are **resources**. These include the full gambit of psychological, physical and demographic potential upon which consumers have to draw. **Resources** embrace education, income, self-confidence, health, eagerness to buy, intelligence and energy level.

Consumers have more **resources** to enjoy between adolescence and middle age. However, the older they get the lower their available resources and the higher their propensity to suffer from depression, poor cash flow as well as physical or psychological impairment.

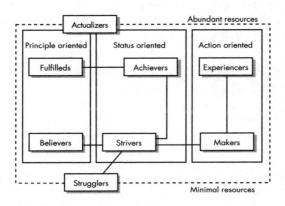

(Reproduced by kind permission of SRI International)

Which VAL should you target?

Actualizers	Independent, leaders, risk takers, fragmented global, complex
Fulfilled	Organized, self-assured, intellectual, well informed, content, open minded, curious
Believers	Literal, respectful, loyal, consistent, traditional, dependable
Achievers	Conventional, brand conscious, pragmatic, diligent, focused, enterprising
Strivers	Eager, social, trendy, approval seeking, image conscious
Experiencers	Impatient, impulsive, spontaneous, creative, rebellious, trend conscious
Makers	Self-sufficient, practical, family oriented, physical, role conscious

Invariably when it comes to research, imaginative marketers develop acronyms even further. Below are a few popular psychographic terms including acronyms, that may help identify *your* target audience.

Sisters are doing it for themselves

Women have long played an important role for marketers. (*See* 'Changing face of the market', page 34.) By the 2000s, men's concerns over their disappearing traditional roles climaxed in their reconsideration of the Men's Movement (launched in the United States in the 1980s). For these unpolitically correct, chest-thumping men, the term **WIFE** was no more than an acronym for Washing, Ironing, Fornicating, Etc. Clearly the movement was unfocused. More importantly, for a few marketers this represented the first seeds of change in politically correct stereotyping of the sexes. Liberation was promised through a rising backlash against women's escalating assertiveness. Although never spoken of in public, this ideal covertly tugged at

Very young	Young/dynamic	Married	Established	Retired
Baby Boomer Originally people who grew up after the 1960s baby boom. Also refers to people born at historic periods of population increase.	**Skotey** Spoiled kid of the 1980s.	**Dinkies** Dual income, no kids, married couple.	**Woopies** Well-off (over 55). Pre-retirement. (AKA Grey Panthers)	**Wrinklies** People in their twenties during Second World War.
	Millennium Junkie Early adopter who wants to change society.	**Empty nesters** Couple, no kids.	**Glams** Greying, leisured, affluent, middle-aged.	**Crinklies** (Same as Wrinklies – see 'New Millennium', page 35)
Baby Busters Born just after *original* Baby Boomers generation so, in the 1990s, had less need of housing and goods.	**Buppies** Black upwardly mobile professionals.	**Managing mums** Guilt-ridden mothers.	**Markas** Middle-aged re-nester, kids away.	**Silver market** People aged 60+.
	Road Warriors Well-travelled executives – usually salespersons.	**Minks** Multiple income, no kids.	**Jolies** Jet-setting, 49–59, free of financial worries.	**Internots** Anti-Webs – cyberphobes.
Curent Boomers 45–55 (Baby boomers who resist 'growing old'. They offer the imaginative marketer a great opportunity to produce youth-oriented campaigns far longer than normal Young/Dynamic. Hence Baby Boomers will often be open to accept youth-culture language and concepts.)	**Crusty** Lifestyle-rough clothes, matted hair.	**Puppies** Previous young upwardly mobile professionals.	**Whannies** We have a nanny.	**Dippies** Dual income pensioners.
	Yuppies Young upwardly mobile professionals.	**Islington Person** Social left-winger.	**Holiday Junkies** 'Hooked' on holidays.	**Farte** Fearful of ageing or retiring too early.
	Y-people (Y-person – Yuppie)	**Foodie** Hobby is food.	**Methuselah market** Rich – 5 years pre-retirement.	**Guppies** Breed guppy fish.
	NETizen Member of Net Heads community.	**Tik** Two incomes with kids.	**Fluffy** Feminine, loving, understanding – faithfully yours – Typified anti-feminist wives of the late 1990s.	
	Cybernaut Surfer.	**Muppie** Middle-aged urban professional.		
Sandwich generation Cares for ageing parents and children.	**Bimboy** Male Bimbo.	**Mouse potato** Hooked all day to the Internet.	**Power Bimbo Killer Bimbo** Careerist, previous Airhead.	
	Grumpies Grim, ruthless, upwardly mobile professionals.	**Media clam** Selectively chooses marketing messages or type of preferred media. The media clam typifies the discerning consumer of the twenty-first century.	**Lombard** Lots of money but a real dickhead.	
	Nummpie New upwardly mobile media person fascinated with New Media marketing (pronounced NU Me Yah).			
	Hoho Happy, optimistic home owner			

the sociological heart strings of males who believed in the law of natural discrimination which postulated that those women who 'could', 'did'; those who 'couldn't' became feminists.

Did you know?
Within the first decade of the twenty-first century in the UK over 12 million new homes were occupied by single owners. Therefore, many single men will also be buying household items like cleaning materials and food.

Corporate participation of intensely marketed, morale boosting, overtly male heterosexual bonding activities, like combat games, is a marketing business tool covering the *people* aspect of the marketing mix. It re-unites team spirit within the enterprise. (See page 52.)

In the press, aggressively male-oriented titles depict women as playthings and men as players. Marketers from computer game companies to fashion houses have a lucrative medium in which to advertise. Fast-moving consumer goods marketers in the UK like Mars, Unilever, Cadbury and Kellogg recognize this and book advertisements in the appropriate titles. By 2005, the success of 'macho marketing' could be measured by the space on supermarket shelves which carry magazines whose editorial is influenced mostly by testosterone agendas rather than political issues. Perhaps, reassuringly, growth of magazines catering for the gay market is also rising.

A woman's most erogenous zone is her mind (Raquel Welch) – A man's brains are in his pants (Anon)

The majority of European countries' populations have more women than men. As we progress into the twenty-first century, this population contrast between the sexes will become even more acute, thereby providing the imaginative marketer with a tremendous market potential.

Marketing in action
Draw up a list of six potential new titles for magazines aimed at the over 65 age group and identify the different characteristics of each title.

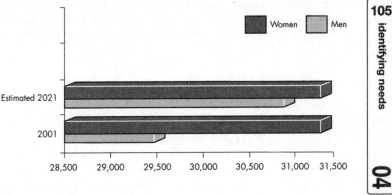

The growth of UK 'girl power' in the twenty-first century

(Source: General Register Offices for Scotland and Northern Ireland)

People call me a feminist whenever I express sentiments that differentiate me from a doormat.

Rebecca West, 1913

Sex in marketing

In the 1980s, feminism 'invented' the New Man who changed nappies in the morning and cried over soppy films at night (whilst bottle-feeding the baby). From the beginning of the 2000s on, marketers encouraged women to become sexual predators. Take, for example, the famous Wonderbra advertising campaign created by advertising agency TBWA. Rather than irritate the women's movement, the ads became icons symbolizing a new, more confident, more controlling woman.

There are certain creative keys when using sex in marketing:

- sophisticated humour
- used as 'the finishing touches' to an already powerful message, rather than the central message
- intelligent delivery
- must be supported by great products or services which at least go towards fulfilling consumer expectations.

Did you know?
The UK's first gay television commercial was broadcast during May 1998 for a deodorant. The creative line was *'Men just can't help acting on impulse'*.

Since biblical times, sex has been held in high esteem in imaginative marketers' 'good books'. Sex sells a message. Rather than being relegated to the traditional British saucy picture postcard humour, sex in the new millennium plays a pivotal role within brand awareness advertising, subtly imparting information which, as time goes by, will be further appreciated by the female rather than in the exclusively male market – a good example of this are youth brands

Just as the ancient Greeks warned against having everything in moderation and nothing in excess, eventually there will be rumblings of serious trouble when attempting marketing to women – or for that matter men – using sexual imagery. The more the public sees overtly sexual images, the more immune they will become to the message. (Remember, to the imaginative marketer the message, rather than just the medium, is 'King'.)

To avoid this communication impasse, imaginative marketers can either make sex more explicit – and so increase the initial titillation but compound the overall effect, or return to Victorian values. As this would all occur within the twenty-first century, it could mean reverting to ideals more than 100 years after they were originally spoken of by the Edwardian suffrage movement.

It's really EC–PC

(A new standard in social targeting)

With all this background to consider, you can appreciate why your own contemporary marketing plans and campaigns need to be more than simply Politically Correct. They also need to be *Emotionally Correct*. In other words, you need to target human motives, social sentiments and personal emotions rather than just civic and class stereotypes.

Did you know?

It is said that one of Coca-Cola's advertising agencies once sent a letter to US magazines offering guidance on the appropriate placing for Coca-Cola ads. A list of inappropriate editorial adjacent to advertising included:

- sex-related issues
- negative diet information (e.g. bulimia, anorexia, quick weight loss)
- political issues
- drugs (prescription or illegal)
- articles containing vulgar language
- religion.

Offering ideals

Returning to more general research issues, have you noticed how pop music programmes are watched mostly by people who aren't old enough to get into a 12a certificate film, let alone a rave? That is because marketing campaigns featuring specific lifestyles often target the lifestyle (including age group/social group, business type and so on) one level social or age group lower than depicted within the marketing collateral. This gives an appropriate audience something to aspire to.

On the other hand, in the fashion business, women aspire to have slimmer waistlines. This is greatly influenced by advertisements showing slender-waisted models. The irony, however, is that the majority of UK women wear size 16 (USA – 14, Europe – 44). It is why, at the end of fashion sales, there are invariably more smaller sizes left over.

Finding your 'little list' (Customer sources)

Commercial marketing lists are widely available from specialist agencies and suppliers called list brokers. You can purchase such lists to include all kinds of targeting information. Be sure that your list is 'clean'. This means it has been updated within the previous six months. According to the Royal Mail, annually, up to 10 per cent of the UK population changes addresses. Therefore, one in ten people on your database may fall from being profit centres to 'gone-aways'. New home-owners are recorded by list brokers on so-called 'B' lists.

Typical targeting lists are broken down by the following mailing segment profiles:

- Age and sex
- Marital status
- Education
- Mortgage status
- Job title
- Housing
- Household type and relationships
- Type of magazines read
- Employment characteristics
- Size of company
- Race and ethnicity
- Place of birth and citizenship
- Types of entertainment enjoyed

- Journey to work
- Standard Industry Classification codes (SIC).

Your best list source, however, is the one hidden in boxes or within computer systems somewhere in your office. I once had a client who made lots of money offering people special discounts on his products. The discounts were made available through coupons attached to the products. Customers completed the coupons, returned them and received a discount voucher for the next purchase. *'That's a great sales promotion technique,'* I told him. *'Tell me, once you sent off the discount vouchers, what did you do with the coupons?'* He explained that the coupons were stored away. What a waste of information!

Another source of information gathering or collecting – with permission – is the coupon at the bottom of an advertisement or part of a direct mail campaign. Coupons should make discreet enquiries of your customers – without over-burdening them with questions. Similarly, you should emphasize that answers should be legible and consistent in order to not over-burden the person deciphering the coupon.

Ensure your prospect completes the coupon in BLOCK CAPITAL letters. List not less than three simple (tick box option) questions which may be useful in future marketing exercises.

For example:

- How many computers do you have in your office
  1–3 ☐ 4 or over ☐
- How many other credit cards do you have? 1–2 ☐
- Which cards? VISA ☐ MASTERCARD ☐ AMERICAN EXPRESS ☐ OTHER ☐
- Have you purchased any IT equipment with your credit card in the last month? Yes ☐ No ☐
- What was the value of the purchase _____ (Please complete)

…Plus, whatever else is applicable to your type of business.

And yet another source of information gathering – with permission – is e-mail data when people sign on for web-generated news and other useful information.

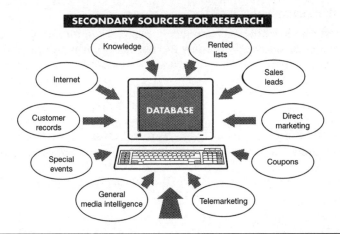

SECONDARY SOURCES FOR RESEARCH

Marketing in action
Draw a flow chart similar to the above, detailing your data sources, referring to specifics (e.g. names of trade exhibitions which you attended, including number of leads generated).

Research methodology

There are many ways to find out about your internal as well as external markets. Whichever you choose, aim to be at least on a knowledge level equal to your competitors. This closes the knowledge gap about your market and so attracts customers towards your business rather than theirs.

Going undercover (more information gathering)

In addition to asking your customers for views, a great source of collecting information is your sales force. Every day your sales team meets and talks to people – prospects who may already be buying from your competitors. The trouble with staff research is that findings may be biased. Recognize that your top sales person will naturally consider how his/her answers will be interpreted in terms of loyalty to the company. Likewise, key managers must be awarded a 'Licence to Drill' suspects for information.

Enterprise information sources

It's surprising how much publicly available imformation you can acquire simply by listening to your wider corporate circle of contacts. Useful *information squealers* include:

- distributors
- agents
- tele-workers
- van drivers
- accountants

- suppliers
- plant workers
- administrators
- receptionists
- you may even be surprised to discover just how much the janitors learn!

You'll also need:

- a 'safe house' to store all your information
- a way to access the information – either manually or electronically (via a data-warehouse, or perhaps barcode reader if, for instance, you are researching stock-related issues)
- an 'A-Team' of senior managers to interpret the information, guide prospectors towards the right direction to collect more data and ensure that findings are acted upon.

In addition to watching your competitors, keep an eye and ear open for what's happening in the market generally. For example, developments in IT may affect the way you service customers in the future. Keep reading, listening and talking to people who thoughtlessly could give you the one snippet of information that could make or break your planned long-term success. As Eleanor Roosevelt put it, '*If we are to live together, we have to talk*,' and taking a parody based on a classic marketing campaign from British Telecom, '*It's good to listen*'.

Impeccable research

1 Consider your objectives. Except in the case of exploratory research, restrict yourself to questions which are directly connected to the objectives.
2 Which research best reveals the answers you need? (Be prepared for conditional conclusions. In other words what you should do if the results veer towards a certain direction necessitating further questions.)
3 Make sure that either you and/or your researcher are fully briefed as to the kind and depth of information sought.

4 Let your researcher know the complete purpose of the research, including the commercial implications of possible findings.

5 Compare findings against previous research studies. (If those interviewed are already conversant with your company, they will give biased answers. Likewise, if your respondents currently deal with your competitors, based on the kind of questions asked and more importantly, the approach and style of those questions, you may actually deter them from giving you business.)

6 Interpret your findings practically rather than purely mathematically.

7 Act upon your research.

Once you have completed each of the seven stages of the research process, plan periodic reviews by exploring changes in the market.

Marketing in action
List your information squealers.

> **FINGLE'S LAW OF INFORMATION**
> The information we have is not what we want.
> The information we want is not what we need.
> The information we need is not available.

In cyberspace, everyone can hear you scream (Research and the web)

The web is a vast pool of knowledge. However, just because something is published on the web, it doesn't automatically follow that it is factual. Prevailing US legislation encourages freedom of speech across all media – including the web. So anyone can e-publish anything as long as it is not overtly pornographic or covertly violent. This said, if you defame someone on the web, wherever the information is viewed – say, China, Spain, Italy ... – it is subject to that country's laws.

As with coupons, the Internet can be used to collect data, however, only with permission from surfers. Being impersonal it immediately does away with a researcher's personal influence on a group. Your website should contain a page which enables people to tell you a bit about themselves.

There are four practical ways to ask a question via the web:

1 **One question at a time.** By revealing only each question in line, you can eliminate problems of respondents being influenced by the following question.

2 **Multiple choice full screen.** In this instance, you reveal all the questions but offer a choice of answers which are selected by dragging down boxes on the screen.

3 **Specific full screen.** As with '2', here you reveal all the questions simultaneously. However, you offer the option for the respondent to complete the answers in full. If you take this route, make sure that outside the United States you let people download the questions, quit the Internet and then re-log on with the answers at a later stage. This saves people expensive 'up-link' (connection) time on the web.

4 **Email.** Send up to 10 specific questions and ask the respondent to email you back the reply. This is the most uncontrolled of the four methods. (As well as impractical, both from a legal and usage point of view.)

General computer-based research is known as Computerized Personal Interviewing (CAPI).

It is becoming common practice to survey large groups of people using laptops. Often the respondent types in answers for himself/herself. Again, the trouble with this method is it raises the spectre of bias. An e-aware person may be happy to type directly on a laptop, thereby lean his/her answers accordingly. On the other hand, a person who is not so PC literate will tend to offer answers more grudgingly.

Insurance companies invariably use Fact-Led research techniques – often using laptop computers. Although complying with industry regulations, these Fact-Led research industry requirements may annoy respondents. The point of this line of questioning is to ascertain that the best advice is given. For example, a Financial Advisor may have to ask repetitive questions such as name, address and current portfolio.

Many contemporary research companies are set up as nationwide panels of correspondents. They regularly complete e-forms about anything from shopping habits to preferred pets. This can be extended further through e-conferencing whereby you can interview panellists via a modem Internet camera link to a network computing device. (Particularly useful if your correspondents are widespread).

All your web information, along with all the other sources, can then be stored in a central electronic data-warehouse which you can cross-reference and 'mine' as you prefer.

Desktop research

There is still a vast source of research available in printed form. So-called 'secondary research' includes a wide pool of information. From trade magazines to national newspapers and CD-ROM directories of companies by industry type, research is consistently being undertaken and reported upon. Business libraries are an excellent source for research. In the UK, members of the Chartered Institute of Marketing, Institute of Direct Marketing and Institute of Directors have access to books, articles and directories covering everything from industry surveys to association listings (you can link to CIM from www.gabaynet.com).

Research, especially statistics, can be likened to witnesses at a trial. Interpreted in a given light, they'll testify for both sides. As with database list buying, make sure the research is relatively fresh. International research can be carried out through record offices, embassies and cultural centres. Key international data includes political yearbooks and forecasts, European Union reports, trade surveys and studies, international marketing statistics, United Nations publications and quango international think-tank studies.

Finally, there is commercial research which can either be purchased as a bespoke document tailored for your needs or via on-going research reports covering industries, buyers, viewers, listeners, and so on.

All desktop and related research should be interpreted with the perspective of what other research indicates as pure 'gut feel'.

Trend research

Desktop research often uncovers tendencies within industries. Superficially, trends may appear, at best, to be mildly relevant to your business and, at worst, just a source of tittle-tattle amusement. However, such trends can provide more than just small-talk around a dinner table. For example, in France, home of culinary cuisine, office workers have steadily abandoned their traditional lunch-time meals at restaurants. Instead, due to pressure of work, they eat at their desks. 'So what?' You may ask. 'We are all busier these days.' Well, if you work within the catering industry or even a related industry, this trend may have more significance than you, or more significantly, your competitor initially notices. For example, if office workers are having their lunch at their desks, does that mean they are eating more sandwiches or cooking meals with an office microwave oven? If it is the latter, a supermarket chain could start to provide special office lunch micro-meals. A microwave manufacturer may want to develop a personal microwave oven. A book publisher may consider producing the office microwave cookbook. A Tupperware company may want to look at the possibility of producing re-useable eating trays which keep the office desk tidy; a fitness company may want to develop a portable exercise machine that can be used at lunch-times in the office and then packed away into a drawer. As you can see, for the imaginative marketer, the possibilities are endless. All you have to do is open your mind and recognize a marketing potential.

Did you know?
French fast food is so 'fast' that around half of the McDonald's chain of restaurants in France feature drive-through facilities.

Marketing in action
List three methods to pose a question via the web and discuss the merits of each one.

Did you know?
In the UK, the average lunch hour is now 32 minutes. According to a Diet Coke survey, men have longer breaks than women – 42 minutes compared to 31.

Primary research

There comes a time when you need to know how much *people* can tell you about a market rather than books or cyberspace. Perhaps you need to measure attitudes towards a market in general.

A quantitative project can be either carefully shaped or completely unstructured. Planned surveys require predetermined questions which are usually answered through preset multiple-choice options. In the case of mailed surveys, there are several important factors to consider.

Steps for mailed (including email or Net generated) questionnaires

1 All research should be unambiguous and unpatronizing. So, explain what's the purpose of the questionnaire. Reassure respondents that answers are confidential. If you intend to use the answers for other divisions within your company, offer the option declining to share data with other related services. (If any division is a separate company, normally, under the Data Protection Act you are prohibited in the UK from sharing data with other companies or businesses.) If specifically requested at the end of the research session, you may offer respondents a sales brochure about the business on whose behalf the research is being conducted. Likewise, you could consider rewarding answers with a free gift. Covert, 'pushy' selling via research isn't just illegal but, from a marketing point of view, stupid. You'll probably alienate more potential customers than recruiting prospects. Overt selling disguised as research is called sugging (a cross between selling and mugging).

2 Make your first question particularly easy to answer. (You don't want to scare people off!)

3 Complete a sample question to show how to answer the rest of the questionnaire.

4 Occasionally, there may be an argument to plan your questions so that they first refer to a concept and gradually build up to a specific product or service that caters for a need. (Once again be wary of sugging.)

5 Ask one question at a time (e.g. **Do you have a pet?** not **Do you have a dog/cat/fish?**)

6 Try, whenever possible, to avoid open-ended questions (e.g. **Could the future be rosy?**)

7 Always use simple words rather than complicated ones (e.g. use **paperwork** not **collateral.**)

8 Whenever possible, avoid leading questions (e.g. **Do you catch the train because it is more comfortable than the bus?**)

9 Don't ask people about subjects of which they obviously have no in-depth knowledge.

10 Don't intimidate your respondent (e.g. **Are you the type of person generally considered by peers as being rather ill informed?** (This is a particularly bad line of questioning. In addition to being intimidating, it is impertinent and irrelevant as the people who should be questioned are the peers – any other answer would be subjective.)

11 Always offer a choice of answers to specific questions, including a **not applicable** option (e.g. **Are you married ☐ Single ☐ Divorced ☐ Separated ☐ Living with a partner None of the above ☐**

12 Be aware of the influence of semantics. Don't use language which reflects your personal views (e.g. In politics, we use **Labour,** not **Left-winger** or **socialist.**)

13 Include a '**Don't know**' option. If the respondent really doesn't have an opinion on a specific question, the person may think it is too difficult to answer and so give up on your entire questionnaire. (*See* 'Posing a general research question', page 120).

14 There are no 'right' answers. Always explain to your respondent that your questionnaire is not an intelligence test. The only thing being assessed is your product or service.

15 Confine your questions to the answers you need, no more. (Don't over-tax your respondent.)

16 Don't cram in any one question the probability of getting a variety of answers.
Rather than...
How many magazines do you subscribe to?
Ask about each of the magazine categories by sector, one at a time and then...
In a month do you buy one ☐, two ☐, three ☐ marketing magazines?
Which titles do you read?
Marketing Herald ☐ Marketing News ☐ Marketing Times ☐

17 If you have to be familiar, do so tactfully.
Instead of
How much do you earn in marketing?

Try...

Is your annual income between:

£12,000–£19,000 ☐ £20,000–£25,000 ☐
£26,000–£30,000 ☐ Over £30,000 ☐

If you just can't avoid confidential questions, explain why you need to ask and clarify:

not

Do you offer your employees tax-free concessions?

instead

To establish how we can provide a discreet, totally professional tax advice service, please answer the following:

Do you offer your employees financial benefits over and above their salaries?

Yes ☐ No ☐

If 'YES', have you sought professional advice that shows some benefits could be 'tax-free'?

☐ Yes ☐ No ☐ Not yet ☐

If applicable, would you be interested in discovering more about 'tax-free' benefits?

Yes ☐ No ☐

Which type of tax advice service do you value most: (This would be a direct-approach survey question as distinct from questions relating to personal impressions about subjects and behavioural attitudes).

☐ **Highly professional**

☐ **One in which you complete forms and an advisor just checks your work**

☐ **One-to-one – very personal**

☐ **One based on extensive experience**

☐ **Standard, 'form-guided'**

☐ **A modern e-commerce led 24-hour service**

In your opinion, what kind of business people are best placed to consult tax advisers? (This typifies an indirect-approach survey question.)

Shrewd ☐   Honest ☐
Crafty ☐   Forward thinking ☐

18 In the case of direct mail, always include a pre-paid envelope for the respondent to return his or her answers confidentially. In the case of direct and indirect surveys via the Internet, always include a confidentiality clause before and after your questions, plus the option in named cases for people to confirm that they wish to participate.

For example in anonymous cases:

This survey is totally anonymous. Survey answers are never written to disk. Plus, of course, we have no idea of your real identity. So please answer honestly.

Did you know?
More than 70 million Americans yearly respond to surveys.

Observational research

If quantity rather than profundity is required from your survey, you need to conduct observational research. This measures how many times people perform tasks rather than why they choose to do so. For example, you can add a visitor counter to your Internet site which records the number of visits or 'hits' you've had. Television companies use a similar method to record the popularity of programmes or commercials. A nationwide group socially representative of the population has its television viewing electronically measured.

Some UK supermarket specialist researchers even equip panels of shoppers with laser-light guided hats. These record which products are most looked at on the shelf and subsequently purchased. Supermarkets can also use electronic scanning equipment at the point of purchase to record the number of products and types sold. Through combining this with data collected from loyalty cards, the imaginative marketer can also research who are purchasing the products and when. The most basic type of observational research – but still effective if the project isn't too large – is simply to watch, write down and then analyse the information in a report.

Quantitative research

This quantifies by measuring in numeric terms and analysed statistically the consumers' behaviour and response to your marketing campaign. It works best with large samples of people who are representative of your proposed target market. Usually, a carefully planned questionnaire is developed which sorts rationalized data into categories and sectors. So, for example, you could calculate how many women per thousand buy a particular type of bra.

If, as can sometimes occur in questionnaire surveys by post or the Net, you fail to get sufficient response from your research, which occasionally happens in any type of questionnaire survey, you should either follow up with a telephone call or polite letters.

Did you know?
Over 75 per cent of UK women wear ill-fitting bras, according to a recent survey. Each woman owned 2.6 bras and ideally would have wished for size 34C. The most popular bra size in the UK is 34B.

Qualitative research

Whereas quantitative research tends to deal with big samples (the bigger the more accurate your results), qualitative research cannot be measured or expressed in numeric terms. So, it is useful to explore 'intangibles' such as feelings and emotions as well as opinions. Therefore, qualitative research restricts itself to small groups or individuals and investigates why people think or behave in a particular way.

Jamie Dow – one of the UK's leading independent market research consultants – specializes in this fascinating area of research. As a facilitator acting on behalf of clients, Jamie leads consumers through a prepared list of topics in a 'depth interview' or group discussion. This encourages people to think laterally, ask and, more importantly, answer questions representing the group's views on a product or service. As the session progresses, so the line of open-ended – as opposed to closed – questioning becomes more focused. In the USA, group discussions are actually called Focus Groups.

Often, sessions are videoed for future discussion within the marketing department. If you intend to hold such a session personally, you may not want the groups to know what product or service is being researched. If they did, answers could be biased. The sessions should be held in a relaxing environment which frees the participants' minds and thereby loosen their preconceptions and inhibitions. This kind of approach also works well with general brainstorming sessions. (*See* 'Brainstorming', page 135 and 'Virtual brainstorming' page 137)

Marketing in action
Summarize the difference between qualitative and quantitative research.

Did you know?
Statistics can be used to stress urgency within a marketing communication. For example, you can remind drivers to: **'Belt up before you drive'**

However, introduce statistics concerning the daily numbers of deaths around the planet caused by bad driving, and you give a far more emphatic warning:

> **Either Belt up this morning or join the other**
> **1,999 road crash FATALITIES who'll be strapped**
> **to morgue tables by tonight**

Based on 1998 figures)

Posing a general research question

Just over halfway through your multiple choice questionnaire, reverse the order of emphasis within your selection of possible answers. This stops respondents becoming indifferent to the style of questioning.

Other forms of research

Syndicated research occurs when you share a general questionnaire with other marketers. You can sponsor as many specific questions as you wish and negotiate to have exclusive rights to the answers.

Mystery shopper research

As the name suggests, here you ask a representative to visit your distributor/retailer to gauge effectiveness. Of course, your agent may have to buy something, so allow for this when budgeting.

Conceptual research

Marketing can be an expensive business. So it pays to test the acceptability of a new campaign or concept before spending vast sums of money promoting it within your marketplace.

From testing the viability of the design of a chocolate bar wrapper to the layout of an advertisement, conceptual research is vital. Media such as television are where conceptual research comes into its own. Because of the budgets it often involves, television companies measure the 'reach' (viewership) of commercials via representative members of the public.

?	Method
How appealing do you find it?	Multiple choice. The beauty of this approach is that you have total control over the questions plus, of course, the survey is relatively easy to turn into a statistical report. The downside is that you can't measure spontaneous observations. (Make sure you graduate the possible answers from one extreme to the other.)
What does this suggest?	Show your respondent a picture or object and ask him/her to 'tick-off' boxes measuring response. (This is often used in conceptual research – interpretation of ink blobs is called Rorschach testing.)
How do you feel?	Respondents have to measure their feelings on a numerical or alphabetical scale.
Do you want it with or without milk?	When you offer an alternative answer – YES or NO, the type of question is called dichotomous. Even if the answer is seemingly YES or NO, still always offer alternatives, NOT SURE or DON'T KNOW.
Who will win?	This encourages people to predict events or issues. If you follow this route make sure that you have provided enough background on the subject either through: (i) relating the leading question to the subject at hand; (ii) confirming that your respondents are suitable.

?	Method
I'll keep it under my hat	This conceals the sort of answers you are after. This ensures totally unbiased replies. Make sure you don't influence answers through the style of question.
I'll give you a clue	This hints at the kind of answers you want. Typically it asks: How do you think... or Where do you believe... or How would you assess... You have to write down the answers to this type of question. So, unless you are a fast writer, or record the conversation, this questioning best helps to determine the sort of subjects to be covered in more specific interviews.
What's the first thing that comes into your head?	Paradigmatic and syntagmatic associations are provocative, free-association psychology-led types of questions. Paradigmatic association is any response to a word stimulus by some semantic link, for example table to chair or boy to girl. In syntagmatic association, responses are much looser, like cloud to white. Adults tend to be paradigmatic.

Television commercials can be especially expensive to produce – let alone broadcast. If you are considering this kind of advertising activity, test the power of your creative approach by:

- presenting your idea for television graphically on a story-board of key 'frames' from the commercial;
- depicting your television commercial animatically through producing a simple animation of your proposed commercial;
- scripting your commercial and get people to read it among a group.

Simulated variable research

This discovers the specific variables which compel consumers to do something (or not). It works only when you are testing specific elements of products or services, whilst ensuring that all other variables don't fluctuate.

For example:

- You could experimentally test the effects of changing the prices on two identical products at identical shop branches. This would tell you whether the increased price would lead to lower sales.
- You could test whether a telephone service is more accessible if a freephone number if offered as opposed to a standard telephone line.

Mood Music Research

A 'classical' example of research in the UK carried out by Leicester University Music Research Group concluded that music affects our choice of food. Depending on the type of music played, diners at a restaurant were either more or less likely to enjoy their meal.

They played three kinds of music followed by the absence of music.

1 Classical music – Vivaldi and Elgar
2 Brit Pop music – Oasis
3 Easy listening music – James Last.

When classical music was played, diners found the food was quite 'sophisticated'. If the music was not conducive to the setting, diners thought they were not getting value for money: they felt the meal was somehow camouflaged.

The more traditionally classical the music, the more diners were prepared to pay. For an average meal when there was no music in the background, diners were prepared to pay £14.30 ($20.00) compared with:

Easy Listening	£14.51	($20.30)
Brit Pop	£16.61	($23.25)
Classic background music	£17.33	($24.25)

(All at 1998/99 prices).

The lower the 'scale', the greater the dissatisfaction about the meal.

Marketing in action

Test the effectiveness of music on your customers by playing different background tracks and comparing general attitudes towards customer service. Which track worked best and why?

Telephone research

Telephone research can be a 'tricky' business. Your main problem is time. People, generally, have too little of it for exercises such as telephone research. However, telephone research is excellent if you want a prompt reaction to something which is about to occur or had recently occurred. This is why so many Opinion Pollsters use the telephone as a rich route towards information.

Another good reason to use the telephone as a research tool is to speak to existing or probable customers. They already know about your organization or your industry sector. So you don't have to waste valuable phone time explaining background details. You could, for example, ask their views about a new service which you plan to introduce. Would it enhance their lives? Add credibility? Save time? Offer flexibility? and so on...

The kind of voice that people hear will also influence their decision to give a few moments of their time to answer questions. Also important is the time of day that you pose your questions, for example:

Morning They may be less busy (if at home).

Lunch-time They may want a break from answering phones – never mind questions!

Close of day They may just want to go home.

Evening They may prefer to watch television or chat with their friends than speak to you. How late should you call? Certainly no later than 9 p.m., unless invited to do so.

Whenever you call, make sure you ask whether or not it is convenient to speak, and if needed, offer a convenient time to call them back.

Don't utter a word until you're utterly compliant

(Tele-marketing and the law)

You also have to consider legal obligations (*see also* 'By the legal book', page 87). For example, it is recommended that you tell people the name of your organization, even ensure that it is printed in a generally available telephone directory. You should explain the purpose of your call and if the person's number was recommended, who provided it. In the UK you can't interview minors, nor can you call ex-directory numbers. Likewise, people who have specifically asked you not to call again should be struck off your list.

If you want to conduct sophisticated, 'high-tech' telephone research, using computerized 'phone calling, make sure that your local legislation permits it. In the UK such automated research has lots of legislative impediments. In most markets, strict data protection rules apply to storing and gaining telephone and contact name details.

Telephone tips

- Don't shout at people!
- Don't talk down to people.
- Explain all relevant aspects of the product or service.
- Allow the person to answer questions without interruption.
- Prepare your questions.
- Consider using a computerized telephone scripting programme to assist with calls.
- Don't whisper.
- Explain the purpose of your questions.
- Don't speak to someone in the office whilst asking questions over the phone.
- Don't offer too many alternative answers to a question.
- Be prepared to be questioned.
- Consider using a specialist telephone marketing company.
- Speak expressively.
- Explain who you are and who you work for.
- Don't intimidate the person.
- Judge whether the person is getting fed up with your questions by the tone of his/her voice.
- Be ready to know to whom to refer a call in the case of unanticipated questions.

- Log calls. Note types of callers most receptive to questions and their future availability.

Marketing in action
Devise a short telephone script to sell a business-to-business answering service. Test it on a colleague and then re-plan it.

One-to-one street interviews

Ask questions to potential consumers about your product or service, perhaps offer samples of, say, your latest chocolate bar, sandwich, drink, magazine and so on, then ask for the consumers' opinion.

More formal street interviews can be harder to conduct. People tend to shy away from interviewers who request 'just a few moments of your time'. At least with trial-and-ask street interviews, interviewees, after examining and trying out a product then answering pertinent questions, can anticipate a reward for their efforts. Irrespective of whether you conduct trial-and-ask interviews or sample interviews, make sure that your research is targeted, simple to understand and manageable. Above all, remember that by posing the right questions and thinking about the consequences of answers, you can find a wealth of untapped opportunities.

Did you know?
Sindy, the doll marketed by Pedigree Dolls and Toys, was named as a result of a street survey. Three alternative names, along with a photograph of the doll, were shown to girls. Cindy, a common name couldn't be trade marked, so the doll was named Sindy.

Empirical research

Empirical research helps to confirm, or otherwise, theories by identifying current or historical trends, views and general insights and then testing and comparing conjecture against facts.

As you have seen, research is a great way to help prepare future developments. But, generally speaking, you can't rely on it as an oracle or soothsayer of all knowledge. So what if your product or service really needs predictive research to succeed? For example, say you manufacture swimwear. Surely it would be useful to know whether or not to anticipate an increased demand for your goods, six months prior to summer? You'd have ample time to schedule production, distribution, packaging, promotions and so forth.

Growth-predictive industries include political forecasts. What occurs within a market's local economy is influenced by national and international trends. This is why typically political predictions are based on measuring swings within the economy. The more extreme the swing, the greater the chances of political change.

Not to be confused with a think tank, the highly respected Henley Centre in the UK is an international consumer consultancy. It recognizes that a real understanding of consumers' fundamental wants, needs and motivations is at the root of creating new revenue streams. The Henley Centre provides a wide variety of research techniques from scenario planning, decision modelling and brand positioning strategies through to market segmentation, pricing analysis and sales forecasting.

In the United States, business-predictive research incorporates many areas. Arguably, one of the oddest must be astrological market research. This uses planetary 'trace' integration to predict market direction, timing and magnitude for either a business sector or financial portfolio.

Summon the 'big guns', get yourself a think tank

Think tanks are more commonly used by governments and lobbyists. However, their findings often uncover invaluable research material to assist specific long-term marketing projects. Such research can be particularly useful for charities seeking new communication messages such as the impending danger of drought, famine and so on. They can also help to identify major possible industry and community needs which may offer new, profitable marketing opportunities.

Some sources for global think tanks include:

• BT Research Laboratories (UK). This is a marvellous centre for predictive research (also known as Futurology). It is acknowledged as Europe's leading telecommunications research and development facility in technology. The Overseas Development Institute is an independent, non-governmental centre for the study of development and humanitarian issues. It provides a forum for discussion of the problems facing developing countries.

- The Arlington Institute (USA) is a policy and research institute which identifies broad-based, emerging national and global trends and events. It was founded by John L. Petersen a futurist and strategic planner specializing in the area of national and global security.
- SRI International describes their think-tank facility as a medium which invents the future through technology innovations. (SRI was responsible for inventing the PC mouse.)

Other eminent think tanks:

- The Confederation of British Industry *www.cbi.org.uk*
- Library of Congress *www.lcweb.loc.gov*
- Foreign and Commonwealth Office Library *www.fco.gov.uk*
- International Planned Parenthood Federation *www.ippf.org*
- International Monetary Fund *www.imf.org*
- European Parliament *www.europarl.eu*
- ASLIB Directory of Information Sources in the UK *www.aslib.co.uk*
- All UK government links to official organizations and sites *www.open.gov.uk*
- Charities Information Bureau (UK) *www.give.org*
- Central Office of Information *www.coi.gov.uk*
- Royal Institute of International Affairs (UK) *www.riia.org*
- Department for International Development (UK) (+44 (0)20 7917 7000)
- Marketing Coaching and Creative Strategies *www.gabay.net.com*

To discover more about central information sources and think tanks, you should approach either a business library, specialist lobby group (for example dealing with old age), trade associations or try accessing the web.

As with all research, think-tank research must be interpreted in the context of your overall objectives and other pieces of research. If you ever get into a situation when you are overwhelmed by the amount of research available for a specific project and are not sure which is best for your needs, use your intuition.

For example, if you intend to open a new restaurant, Chinese or Indian, but can afford to research only one market, opt for the one your 'gut-feeling' tells you is most appropriate. Finally, ensure that your main avenue of research reflects the feelings and thoughts of potential end-users of your product or service. After all, it's what *they* think that really counts.

05

some of the greatest imaginative thinkers

In this chapter you will learn about:

- steps to becoming more creative
- Moses Maimonides
- John Locke
- Aristotle – the father of imaginative marketing?

Now you have fathomed where to find the indicators for your 'brilliant' marketing campaigns, consider the natural source of ideas spurring your imagination.

Over the centuries, humans have pondered over the question of 'What precisely, is an idea?' In my book *Teach Yourself Copywriting* (*see* 'Taking it Further'), I explained how the Greek philosopher Plato (427–347 BCE) argued that the senses (touch, taste, sight, smell, hearing) form the basis for reality. Ideas come about through either direct or indirect connection of one set of facts with another. So, according to him, to get an idea you need to have had some sort of experience through the senses of something connected to the idea. Once you have thought of that idea, even if it doesn't exist, for you, it is real.

Test it: Envisage a mouse in your mind. Now picture an elephant. The mouse squashes the elephant. Try to imagine that scenario. What if I told you that the mouse is driving a steam roller. Or that the mouse and elephant are cartoons. Or the mouse is gigantic and the elephant is tiny? If any of these suggestions help you to picture this image, then such images for you are real.

Five steps to becoming more commercially imaginative

1 **Brainstorming**   In which two heads are better than one (*see* 'Brainstorming', page 135).

2 **Analyse**   every part of a problem in detail – a most laborious approach.

3 **Get inspired**   by the world around you – a form of synectics.

4 **Gut feeling**   Go with a hunch, think 'upside' down, rather than just logically.

5 **Bench marking**   Study another organization – even not directly competitive to yours and pick out the best aspects of its service/process.

The four doors towards creativity

Design agencies often refer to the House of Creativity. The house has four rooms. Each represents an inspirational approach towards answering a creative brief.

The Room of Great Works contains outstanding examples of design from a variety of sources.

The Room of Reason contains hard facts and figures relating to the project in hand.

The Room of Precedent contains previous examples of work either by the company and/or competitors.

Once you have entered every other room, the empty Room of the Unknown, offers infinite space to be as imaginative as you wish.

Cogito Ergo Sum (I think therefore I am)

Réné Déscartes (1596–1650), regarded by some as the 'father of modern-day philosophy', argued that true knowledge comes from pure human reasoning alone. Therefore, you don't even need to have prior sensory experience – even related to the subject in hand, to have an original idea.

From simple thoughts come complex ideas

John Locke (1635–1704) suggested that ideas are based solely on experience. According to Locke, a newly born baby is rather like a blank sheet of paper. As the child develops so the sheet is filled with information acquired through experience.

The adult, according to Locke, experiences two kinds of ideas:

• Ideas of sensation (seeing, hearing, smell, sight, taste) which he called simple ideas;
• Ideas of reflection (deliberation, construction...) which he defined as complex ideas.

He said that simple ideas are based on experience whilst complex ideas combine those experiences to create abstract concepts.

Aristotle's influence on imaginative marketing is immense. He devised a classic process of deductive logic. He perfected the syllogism – a logic argument structure comprising two major premises, followed by a conclusion. The major premise states, 'All Xs are Ys, no Xs are Ys, or some Xs are Ys'. The minor premise highlights a more specific relationship, and the conclusion is predetermined by the form of these premises. For example, 'All marketers are ambitious. I am a marketer, so I am ambitious.'

I market fresh
strawberries

Kids enjoy the snow

Why not market
strawberry ice-cream?

Simple ideas

Simple ideas

**Complex
(abstract ideas)**

Similarly, a blind person recognizes shapes through touch alone. In regaining his/her sight, the person will still distinguish the shapes without the need to touch them. Likewise, as a marketer, you should be able to communicate a compelling marketing concept through powerful creative imagery, without your target audience having prior direct knowledge of it. Those richly complex ideas form part of the currency of imaginative marketing.

From Moses to Moses, there will never be another Moses

Long after his death in 1204, Moses Maimonides (born 1135 in Cordova, Spain) continued to influence imaginative thinkers from all walks of life. Maimonides argued that imaginative thinkers could be categorized as follows:

- **Philosophers** People whose rational abilities are particularly developed and are inspired by a higher (active) intelligence but whose vivid imagination is lacking.
- **The brightest thinkers** People with a highly developed level of intellect as well as vivid imagination.
- **Administrators/bureaucrats/politicians** People with an acutely developed imagination but poorly refined intellect!

Generally speaking, according to Maimonides, the more developed your imaginative skills, through anthropological and spiritual study, the better your ability to recognize original ideas readily even if ambiguously, as distinct from letting them inadvertently pass you by.

And as for the common reaction that people first have when hearing an original idea: 'I'll sleep on it', Maimonides contended that imaginative thinkers, like prophets, capitalized during the time when the brain was most 'creative', during sleep.

The late Sir Isiah Berlin argued that ideas could not be divorced from people and their psychological and cultural milieu. In his book *Two Concepts of Liberty*, Sir Isiah wrote

> When ideas are neglected by those who ought to attend to them – that is to say, those who have been trained to think critically about ideas – they often acquire an unchecked momentum and an irresistible power over multitudes of men.

Today, it is generally regarded that an idea is an episode created in the mind and based on real experience or known facts.

Marketing in action

Which is true?

1 You don't need any specific experience about something to be imaginative.

2 Ideas come only from experience.

Now answer why each one is true or not.

Still stuck? Throw a dinner party

Have you ever planned an imaginary dinner party with your favourite guests like movie stars or singers? Now imagine that you invited your all-time favourite thinkers to help solve a marketing dilemma. Imagine how each would contribute to the situation. Write down their ideas – you'll be amazed by the results.

Life in space? Next you'll be saying there's ice on the moon!

Powerful marketing ideas can be likened to arrays of stars, revolving in an ever-expanding galaxy of creative potential. An imaginative marketer finds ways to connect and spin seemingly different constellations into an elegant Milky Way, abundant with innovative thoughts.

Once those thoughts are correlated, through the use of communication tools (the marketing mix) in essence you transplant those ideas into the minds of your target audience(s).

Eureka! Examples of idea fusion

Johann Guttenberg (c. 1400–66) fused the mechanics of a wine press with a coin punch and invented the printing press.

Isaac Newton (1642–1727) fused the movement of waves with falling apples and discovered gravity.

Percy Shaw of Halifax, England, fused the effects of light reflecting on a cat's eye and poor visibility caused by fog and invented the Catseye road studs.

Marketing in action
Through combining unrelated objects, what new object could you invent (however far fetched or fantastic) and which media would you choose to promote it?

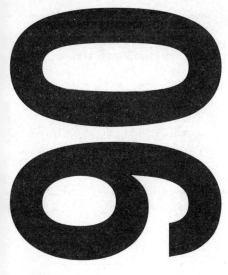

06

brainstorming

In this chapter you will learn about:
- brainstorming
- conceptual charting
- cultivating ideas

If your ideas are all dried up, get soaked

Brainstorming generates long lists of potential marketing opportunities. The more intensive the brainstorm session, the greater your potential source of ideas.

The brainstorming process

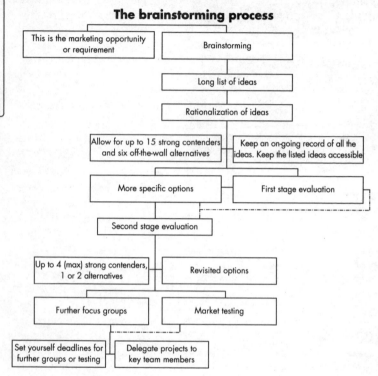

The most effective brainstorming sessions comprise people who, in addition to the core development team, may have no direct experience of a particular product/service or the company developing it.

All brainstorming sessions start quite laterally and narrow in definition as they progress.

Just as it is best not to exclusively include immediate team members in your brainstorm, so it is essential to have an independent facilitator acting as as chairperson and encouraging free thought, without also bringing the added burden of any political agenda.

As I discuss in my book *Teach Yourself Copywriting* (*see* 'Taking it Further') brainstorming is best conducted outside normal working premises. Since the first edition of that book was published, my company, Gabay has developed a particularly effective mode of brainstorming, designed for the twenty-first century, called Virtual Brainstorming™. Here, led by a trained market researcher with psychological marketing skills, Brainstormers who make up a synectics-led Focus Group (originally developed in Harvard) are invited to 'step into' a surreal world appropriate to the subject being brainstormed. Then they are led through a highly structured method of rationalizing their thoughts.

Being a chimerical environment, a Virtual Brainstorming™ session can be conducted anywhere your imagination can conceive, from a jungle to the top of a mountain, provided the location enhances imaginative thought and group dynamics energy.

Did you know?
Velcro was invented as a direct consequence of a brainstorming session involving weeds with burrs in a jungle.

I have no idea what you are talking about

In my travels as a marketing strategist and coach, I get to hear lots of excuses why brainstormed ideas may be impractical for a company. Most are invalid. Be forewarned of the following top ten defences, based on *Teach Yourself Copywriting*, against what may really be a terrific idea.

Ten motives for ideological assassination

1 It's too expensive.
2 It will never work – although I can't say why.
3 Not my responsibility.
4 We're too busy.
5 The public won't buy it.
6 We have to put profits before people.
7 If we still like the idea in a couple of months, we'll look at it again.

8 The Managing Director's husband will never approve.

9 It sounds too innovative.

10 If your idea has been brutally assassinated, leaving blood on the hands of more than one suspect, the accomplices probably suggested this idea killer – *Why don't we form a committee?*

Did you know?
The people you mix with directly affect your imaginative potential. Avoid Energy Thieves keen to dismiss ideas. Mingle instead with Idea Cultivators who encourage success.

Guidelines for effective brainstorming

Just as there are ways to smother a refreshing breath of an idea at birth, so there are guidelines which encourage ideas to flourish.

1 No brainstormer can judge another brainstormer's suggestions.

2 Every brainstormer is equal.

3 The more off-the-wall an idea is the better.

4 All ideas can be combined and **positively** enhanced.

5 Brainstormers should make fun their priority and in doing so, break down work-barriers

6 Don't attempt to solve problems step by step. Try more lateral methods.

7 Consider every alternative.

8 Don't stunt the growth of an idea by brainstorming in a dull or restrictive environment. (A good case for Virtual Brainstorming™.)

9 Encourage brainstormers to get to know each other, and so speak more openly.

10 Ask your brainstormers to 'leave' their job titles and status by the door before entering the brainstorming environment.

11 Restrict your troops of brainstormers to no more than 14 people per group.

12 Brainstorm sessions should generate a long list of ideas; however good or bad they appear.

13 Include every idea in the final list. To censor ideas is to prejudge them.

14 Brainstormers cannot ask leading or intimidating questions, for example 'Surely you agreed that when it comes to actual experience of the subject, you should leave the thinking to professionals – like me?'

15 Whether a marketing idea sounds good or odd, be curious to develop it further.

16 Once you have all agreed on the most accurate and informed creative options, let the final analysis take pure 'gut-feeling' or intuition into account.

Did you know?
Imaginative marketers really do let their hearts rule their heads: the heart produces at least twice the amount of electricity as the brain.

Are you lonesome tonight?

What if you don't have anyone to brainstorm with? Excluding the possibilities that you are anti-social, have bad breath and so on, I still suggest that you find someone with whom you can thrash out your ideas.

If your enterprise is very modest, you could ask friends and family or even consider holding an interactive brainstorming session on the Net (especially if conducted via webcams and so letting you keep the all-important eye contact going).

If on the other hand you intend to brainstorm in groups, remember that ideas should compete against each other rather than allowing personalities to take up the gauntlet. Also, all brainstorm groups should include leaders, followers and neutral-minded people. Don't allow one to dominate another.

Feeling lost? Design a better route towards ideas

So now you have produced reams of fascinating ideas and research. How do you intend to make head and tail of it all? One highly imaginative method to help interpret your ideas is to become an architect of ideas.

Conceptual charts turn idle doodles on a piece of paper into visions. (N.B: Spider diagrams are web-shaped hexagonal shapes which help categorize your ideas into clusters.)

Like an architectural blueprint of individual towns, the way you arrange and connect the thoughts in your chart may be quite different from mine. Conceptual charts let you transfer those 'thinking' routes on to paper. They segment your ideas into distinctive areas (like the shopping mall, local school, church and so on). All these places similar to 'B' roads, emanate and divide from a central need or goal which can be compared to the town square or piazza.

Conceptual charts help you to deal with lots of complex projects simultaneously. Now, of course, one could list each idea as it comes. But although nice and neat, it's too restricting and instantly censors which ideas should go under which list. There is literally no space on the chart for an idea to bloom.

Incredibly, up to 95 per cent of your time can be wasted trying to recollect words which have no real bearing on your memory. When those words are commercially significant you need to be able to distinguish between propositions which can all too easily become 'muffled' by linking words and sentences separating them. Making logical connections with the potential to lead to brilliant new marketing concepts, can become difficult.

Similar to doodles on a scrap of paper, complete your chart as you 'dream up' possible routes. (As discussed in 'Braintyping', page 95, the mind doesn't think vertically – it imagines laterally.)

'Roads' from the centre of your conceptual chart can be drawn in colour (like in a geographic map denoting 'A' roads from highways): one colour per specific subject, per route. The roads may be sign posted like street indicators at intersections with simple pictures summarizing a concept. The more ideas you have the more roads you build until you design a bustling city, brimming with potential.

A ten-minute conceptual chart based on the word 'imagination'

07

under the microscope – taking a closer look at your business

In this chapter you will learn about:
- the emotional sales point (esp)
- making your brand distinctive

Unique Sales/Selling Propositions/Points

Throughout this book, you have learnt about the importance of establishing a Unique Selling Proposition or Selling Point (USP). Ironically, most USPs are fallacies, in that in essence there isn't just one selling point about a product or service. For the imaginative marketer, every product or service contains a wealth of selling propositions. The real challenge is to narrow those USPs to the most appropriate for each marketing message.

For example, you may want to market a new confectionery sweet bar. Depending on your market, your message would be tailored accordingly. So for children, the USP characteristic may be that your bar is particularly chewy. If so, it can be compared to enjoying the texture of a traditional wine-gum. To a health-conscious market it may be that the bar is made with low-fat milk. Or that, in addition to being more healthy for your diet, it is also healthy for your muscles as, being chewy, each time you eat it you naturally exercise your jaw.

It is important to remember that tactical communication USPs should never confuse or diffuse the core USP benefit of your larger brand.

Which nibble do you fancy the most?

On Valentine's Day (14 February) I like to present Michelle, my wife, with a box of delicious chocolates. (Read this as either 'old fashioned' or someone who just wants a peaceful life!) Forrest Gump is accredited as saying that 'life is like a box of chocolates', so too, are USPs like a variety box of sweets. How do you choose your favourite, best suited for your tastes?

Michelle instinctively opts for the Strawberry Creams, as she appreciates their taste and consistency. That leaves me with Nougat – chewy; Walnut – crunchy; Toffee – long lasting; Cherry brandy – very sweet; Double chocolate – rich and smooth, and finally, Almond whip – crumbly shell on the outside, light inside. I like something which is sweet and enduring. So I look for chocolates which offer those kinds of USP qualities. Then I start to subdivide the selection into suitable choices. Similarly, you can split your USPs into main headings and subdivide into three or so distinctive features.

It soon becomes apparent that some of those subdivided features are similar to others. So you dispose of the lesser benefit-led options and keep the others. The fewer your choice of possible USPs at the beginning, the sooner you'll arrive at your definitive USP.

Just to add objectivity, consider showing your final selection to someone or a group not directly involved with the project. If it really boils down to you to choose, remember that the features should be aimed towards what your potential customers stand to gain, rather than the more obvious advantages for your enterprise.

Tactical USPs for vertical marketing programmes should never be confused with the USP which forms part of your main brand. This kind of USP has to remain consistent. It is from this powerful core proposition that all other forms of communication develop. (*See also* 'Types of brand', page 147.)

Planning Director, Danielle Aarons, explains USPs as follows:

> Every marketing company is in pursuit of the elusive USP. The best USP is compelling and motivating. The Body Shop, for example, clearly identified the opportunity for a pro-animal welfare, environmentally sensitive, range of body-care products. This USP was not only unique in its time, but highly relevant and compelling to socially aware consumers.

> USPs are often short lived. Before you know it, competition moves in to address the gap (see Ansoff). The challenge for imaginative marketers is to own that gap and through positioning, ensuring that the brand, product or service best meets consumer needs. Positioning as a marketing technique doesn't occupy a piece of paper, rather it occupies the minds of consumers. Now, if as an imaginative marketer, you go ahead and make statements or promises about your brand, you can be pretty sure that your consumers will subconsciously say to themselves, '**go on, prove it**'. Consumer intelligence, through market research, helps provide the competitive edge as can a commitment to update a product, its packaging and advertising to address the changing needs of consumers.

Another view on USPs

So far I have discussed the use of USPs within traditional marketing 'textbook' terms. However, more often than not, your product or service won't have any attribute which can truly be described as Unique.

Come to think about it, there are not that many things which can honestly be called unique. Further still, the word 'Unique' is probably one of the most misused terms banded around in marketing.

Grammatically and factually, you cannot say that your product or service is 'virtually unique' or 'quite unique'. Simply, there are no shades of uniqueness. The exception to the rule may perhaps be attributed to twins who can be 'almost unique' or 'virtually unique'. So, unless you are marketing a fertility procedure, you would be best advised to stay away from 'unique' in your marketing copywriting.

Having established that you should steer clear of 'unique', you need to find an alternative. You could try either 'Current' Sales Proposition or 'Greatest' Sales Proposition or even 'Targeted'. Your **Current Sales Proposition,** like a mission statement, should be allowed to evolve naturally and in compliance with market forces. Your **Greatest Sales Proposition** should take into account the finest of all the benefits and features. Your **Targeted Sales Proposition** (alternatively **Extra Value Proposition** or **Appropriate Marketing Proposition**) should be directed towards individual (vertical) markets most appropriate for tactical campaigns.

Most important of all, your brand should feature an ESP – emotional sales point. This powerful approach tackles one of the most fundamental of all marketing strategies – namely, appealing to the fact that people often think with their heads but act with their hearts. In fact, without an ESP, your brand marketing remains lifeless.

Marketing in action

List the USPs of your car, then list the TSPs for these drivers.

a) A busy housewife with kids
b) A student
c) A harassed marketer.

08
image is everything

In this chapter you will learn about:
- brand types
- bringing your brand to life
- brand management

Does your surname instil a sense of pride? How about individual members of your family? Brothers, sisters, uncles, aunts and so on? When you think about their character and how they represent the family, how do you feel?

Those values are like brand values. Feelings fire up emotions, beliefs and attitudes identifying you with an individual's personality. Such intimacy is essential in marketing. Simply by knowing that a product or service originates from a specific 'brand' name, a consumer has a hunch as to whether or not it is likely to be the sort of thing worth acquiring or investigating further.

Just as your immediate family unit is probably linked to a parent couple, so many businesses are linked to a parent brand name which may embrace, inspire and drive a group of divisional organizations.

Types of brands

Family brands

These feature company names such as Cadbury, Lever, Heinz, etc.

Product line brands

These feature specifically created subsidiary brand names (e.g. *Teach Yourself*, Homebase, Do It All, etc).

Umbrella brands

Here, the main family brand is used to endorse a specific sub-brand (e.g. Cadbury's Snack, Elite Instant Coffee, McVitie's Go Ahead, Heinz Big Soup, etc).

Individual brands

These feature specific brand names (e.g., Rice Krispies, Cheerios, Persil, etc). Keep in mind that individual products and services may come and go (through the natural course of their Product Life Cycle), the master brand, however, goes on and on...

Own-label brands

Middlemen or dealers may also put their names to a brand – often referred to as private brands or wholesaler's brands. For instance, a major retailer may include its name on labels (also known as own-label brands), for example Better Buys Baked Beans, Corner Shop Cola, etc. When groups of retailers market own labels, the brand is sometimes referred to as a distributor's brand. As Simon Lowden, former Marketing Manager at Pepsi Cola UK told me:

> There will always be a role for cheap brands in a repertoire in terms of branded colas in the UK, people don't tend to be brand loyal, they generally drink by habit and repertoire.

It's important that you don't associate own-label brands with consumers who simply want to save a few pennies on products. For example, it is commonly known that in certain cases, dieters may purchase own-label brands as opposed to mainstream brands. Some argue that this is simply because psychologically they want to feel deprived of enjoying 'the best'.

Own brands shouldn't be confused with cases in which a retailer not directly associated with a major brand sells it at a discounted price (such as a supermarket selling branded jeans cheaply). In such instances, it is reported that the European Court of Justice set a precedent that the supermarket is allowed to advertise the branded goods as long as the advertisement doesn't '*seriously* damage the reputation of the trade mark'.

Virtual brands

In this case, the brand owner doesn't actually handle any production process. Instead it is conducted by an outside supplier. (Richard Branson's Virgin Cola is one such example.)

Just because consumers go for a lesser-known cola, it doesn't necessarily follow that they also opt for other lesser-known brands as well. As you've seen in the section on research, human intellect is *far* more complicated.

Web brands

In the early days of the dot com boom, these were rapidly developed through the Internet and may enjoy short-lived PLCs (*see* Product Life Cycles, page 18). Because the Internet is highly scaleable, both small and international companies compete equally over the web, which history has shown can lead to little small trader 'bangs' going 'boom' and big corporation 'booms' going bust. Therefore, making your brand distinctive becomes even more important. This requires consistent promotion through all supporting media as well as the web, especially as traditional webvertising opportunities like banner ads are becoming increasingly unsuccessful. (*See* E-commerce, page 209.)

Brand marketing

With so much at stake, marketing a brand name and so explaining its set of perceived values can be of equal, if not greater, importance as marketing a specific material product or service. In fact, it is safe to say that in marketing terms values may be equal but nothing is bigger or better than your brand.

Brand marketing is much more intricate than simply identifying a commercial name or putting a logo on a piece of packaging. It's a bit like an impressive magic trick in that it's not just what you see that fills you with awe but what you can't see. But imagine and associate with the entire experience. Based on the power and conviction of a mission statement, (*see* 'Mission Statement', page 45) brand marketing touches every facet of the marketing mix. It can be recognized and so measured in the congruity of an overall marketing communication plan from the shape of packaging to the design of a website, the style of an advertisement, its design, packaging, targeting and copywriting.

Forget brand promise – think 'BrandAction'

From airlines to cornershops, if your brand promises an ideal, you have to be seen to pursue it rather than pay it lip-service. Through not doing so you invariably alienate the target audience your brand is trying to attract.

Just as you can't fully judge a person by face value alone, so people identify allegiances with brands according to their ability to gain early association with the brands concerned on distinctive levels. (Rather like Maslow's Pyramid – *see* 'Maslow', page 91.)

> **Did you know?**
> Every marketing message needs conviction – without it, there is no substance. Follow the **AIDCA** rule: **Attention** leads to interest. **Interest** leads to desire in a product or service. **Desire** leads to convincing the audience that what they want, they *really* can afford. **Conviction** leads to action to buy.

Level one – My brand is irresistible

Brands are in a way like religious icons, in that they help people to assert their feelings. So consider your customers at every stage of the development of your brand.

I once visited a church in Bethlehem, Israel. Each of its many stained-glass windows featured a picture of Christ as interpreted by individual countries. There were Afro-deities, Asian deities, Western deities... As I looked around I saw that specific portrayals of Christ had particular effects on visitors. One spurred a tourist to identify Christ with very 'mortal' attributes. Another tourist had tears running down her face as she obviously felt Christ's 'divinity'.

Brands, too, should provoke people to recognize evocative, instinctively exceptional qualities which they would want others to recognize admirably in them.

Level two – My brand achieves all this...

At an early stage, people want to know how well an individual, family or umbrella brand of products/services performs. How is the foundation brand supported and who developed it? This is often expressed by encapsulating a brand's benefit in a single practical statement. This statement may not be especially distinctive from that of a competitor. However, it is emphatically distinguishable within a broad marketplace. Examples: 'Apple computers are stylish, fast and efficient.' 'British Telecom lets people communicate.' 'Dell Computers are tailored to your needs.'

Level three – My brand is different

If taken out of context, this level in essence is the hardest to communicate. However, once it has the support of the other two, it becomes immensely potent and socially, if not secularly, politically and culturally enlightening. These levels of brand marketing are typically interpreted through music, depiction of group values (such as professional ideological, family, ethnic, sexual or religious) as well as with emotive photography and illustration.

With all the 'legs' of your brand standing firmly, your brand attracts customer loyalty as consumers return time and time again to become clients. Brand loyalty relies on a core set of strengths and values that never change. These often include quality, people, service, distribution and customer care.

This said, if your brand is meant to be perceived as being 'trendy', after a while of continuous exposure it can, if not handled properly, start to be regarded as part of the establishment rather than something continuously and refreshingly alive. Which is why drawing on the brand's core strengths and beliefs, it's values adapt to market needs. This would typically apply to fashion and music businesses. It could also apply to David and Goliath companies. (David initially representing the 'new kid' on the block – such as Richard Branson, Bill Gates, etc., whilst 'Goliath' is the aged corporate giant.) Or even political parties promising a lot but delivering a little. Even if your brand is not meant to be valued in those terms, you should still be wary that consumers as a whole are increasingly sophisticated. Therefore, your brand has to be consistently relevant for a target audience.

Brands which fall in this category include rebel brands promoted as anti-establishment. Theme-style restaurants may be considered in this category.

Marketing in action
What is the difference between an own-label and a family brand?

Going global

In time, your brand adopts values which are recognized and appreciated globally. Subdivisions of your brand (family brands, etc.) extend and adapt those values and needs of specific localized types of consumers and markets.

Chris Holt, the former Head of Design Management at British Airways, takes up the brand extension story.

> Profit is often down to yield. In airlines the bigger yield comes from the front end of the aeroplane. The contribution to the bottom line is much less per passenger

in World Traveller cabins at the back than premium ones at the front. So you have to ask yourself how else can we attract more profitable customers whilst keeping them satisfied?

Part of our marketing strategy is to stretch the brand into an experience beyond just the aircraft seat. After all, the customer encounter of the company isn't simply about sitting in an aeroplane, but either side of that. Stretching the brand is about enhancing the travel experience. Whether it's insurance, medical services, ground transportation, hotels, holidays, theatre tickets, shopping and airport lounges, tailor-made packages for business travellers... it all counts. As long as the brand extension is directly related to core it is worth exploring.

Over here, over paid – over your head

In addition to the benefits of nurturing specific types of customer relationships, the beauty of extending international brand values and to adapt to the needs of localized consumers is that a local division of a conglomerate can nurture poignant, provincial values whilst also gaining international esteem. Moreover, a big international brand name can help local divisions in their regional negotiations to manufacture or produce goods and services. The downside of this is that without the right kind of brand management, your imaginative creative campaigns may become stifled by restrictions imposed by a head office in another country. This kind of decentralization is typical in a global market. The result is that you spend more time trying to appease HQ marketing departments whilst less time actually getting on with the business of promoting and unifying your brand values and positioning.

The tail wags the dog

Irrespective of globalization, if you extend your local brand across too many sectors – for example, a fashion brand used on everything from toiletries to watches, records, sunglasses, wallets and stationery, and so on – you face a real confrontation through overstretching your brand so much that all your goodwill and equity snap back in your face.

Now, if you are beginning to think that all this 'globalization' stuff isn't really applicable to your own branding exercise, think again. A really great brand doesn't initially have to be measured purely in terms of its international standing. It may not be practicable. Brand values relate to how customers distinguish you, your awareness within the market and customer credibility/reliability. Whether yours may not be the final choice, but the most prestigious and so first name that comes to mind (mind share). This last aspect is the foundation for your long-term branding success, for if you can turn a satisfied customer into a willing advocate for your brand, your acquired values will spread far and wide and as fast as the speed of a customer's recommendation by the Net, in person and by phone. (*See also* 'Integrated solution providers', page 205.)

Did you know?
A US baby-food manufacturer featured a baby on its African food labels. Sales were low. They didn't realize that in Africa, labels were meant to depict a product's contents.

Many imaginative marketers take advantage from competitive global branding simply through defending their own locally produced products against mega-sized international brand names. In India, for example, Mohun's Corn Flakes re-launched and improved their corn flakes market with notable success in a direct challenge to Kellogg's. Likewise, a locally marketed North Indian fast-food chain enjoyed a 20 per cent increase in sales the year Pizza Hut, McDonald's and Domino's Pizza entered the Indian market.

The brand egg

Imaginative marketers may like to think of brands in terms of an egg. The yolk represents the brand's core strengths, whilst the white represents its supporting values and the shell the external, thereby 'first sight', contemporary perceptions.

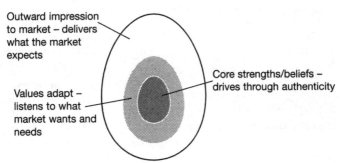

The brand egg

Other variations on the brand egg include the **brand triangle** in which the base forms the foundation of the brand, the middle is divided into segments supporting the basic values and the tip, like an aerial, transmits the most accessible values and features to a target audience.

A further variation is the **brand volcano**. Here each level of a brand's heritage solidifies over time so re-enforcing and enriching its heritage and value.

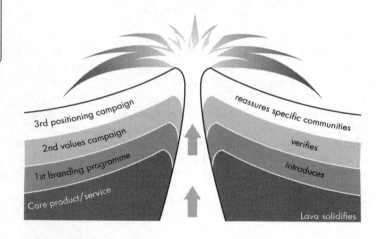

The brand positioning volcano

Chris Holt fetchingly summarizes brand value as a way of identifying something and relating to it.

> Every person has a personality that brings the individual to life. That personality is unique to that person. Think of this person's total self as a 'brand', you would take into consideration his personality and the way he presents himself. This value has an invisible inheritance, being whatever spiritual or emotional aspects that make up the 'brand'. Likewise, a major brand enjoys a singular personality enhanced by the additional features making up the brand 'shell'. Your personal 'shell' includes your voice, hair style, choice of clothes and personality. The added features – the equivalent of how you wear your hair, your style of shirt, spectacles, tie and so forth – help people determine how the outer shell reflects the inner man.

A corporation of any kind and size is a bit like that. You have the spiritual and emotional relationship with the brand. Then there are the specific products or services and the way in which they are packaged and presented.

Brand extent	Brand magnitude	Brand sway	Brand affinity	Brand sensitivity
Development into new pastures as well as brand stretching into related product/ service areas without compromising the core potency of a brand's original set of values.	Supremacy in terms of esteem rather than purely apportion within a market sector.	The relative significance of personal association the brand attracts from various segments of the market, including the internal market (employees and share-holders).	The allegiance and admiration the brand attracts from existing as well as potential customers.	The level of feeling and emotions evoked by the brand.

Did you know?
Brand management, as a marketing system, was introduced by Proctor and Gamble in the 1930s.

09 branding in action

In this chapter you will learn about:
- understanding local
  perceptions
- brand icons
- origins of some of the world's
  most famous brands

What do the late Diana, Princess of Wales, Nike shoes, British Airways, Pepsi Cola and an eighteenth-century French prisoner all have in common? From a marketing perspective they all possess a powerful feature – their perceived value.

Nike, in contrast to its fame, hardly owns any tangible assets like manufacturing equipment. Yet its brand is one of the most valued across the globe and is strongly associated with an individual's potential to win. (The company's slogan is 'Just Do It'.)

British Airways is internationally recognized, in terms of mind share at least as the global ambassador for the UK.

Pepsi Cola is a globally respected brand which tends to align itself with popular music and therefore youth culture. This creates a target market affinity.

> The youth market drinks more cola than any other section of the market. They drink more carbonated drinks per head. (In traditional demographic terms: from the age of 11 through to about 19/20.)

> Successful advertising like Levi's might and Nike appeals to a broad age range of people. Dad may wear an Adidas track suit and want to get the Sunday morning papers. Yet you still have a six-year-old kid demanding expensive Nike trainers for his birthday because they are *the* trainers to wear. Once you get the youth mind-set, you capture a high ground.

Revolutionizing perceptions

What of that French prisoner? Imagine it is the 1790s. The French aristocracy have kept a group of peasants chained in underground dungeons. The prisoners see only shadows. After a while, those shadows shape their perception of the world. Then, a prisoner escapes and steps out into the colourful daylight. He sees the world has texture and shade which provide new meaning to him. The prisoner returns to liberate the others. His eyes remain dazzled by natural light. Upon seeing his bewildered expression, the other prisoners mistake his rantings about a new outlook on life for lunacy. So it is that, in marketing, perceptions have to be shaped through a realistic communications plan in a way that is as clear as daylight even for those who see nothing but shadows.

Diana – a legacy of hope

Years after her death Diana, Princess of Wales' name is still perceived as having a humane quality. As a universally adapted icon it is so powerful and, from a branding perspective, valuable that marketers fall over one another to capitalize upon its prestige.

Within the first six months of her tragic death in August 1997, Diana memorabilia had netted over £100 million ($146 million) worth of business for companies. To protect her image and name, the Princess of Wales Memorial Fund was created and the official 'Diana' logo registered. Businesses featuring the logo could thereby add a sense of solemnity and authenticity to their product. The logo featured three important attractive marketing devices:

- Diana's personal signature
- Diana's personal favourite colour – purple
- 'Official' support through the caption: 'Princess of Wales Memorial Fund'.

Just as people felt they 'knew' Diana in life, so, through the combination of the three powerful marketing logo devices, it was intended that they would be drawn closer to her in memory.

Diana's good name and memory became in danger of being devalued by the market. For example, tacky T-shirts were sold with a legend that read: *'Born a princess, died a saint, now an angel'*. Mintel research, reported in the trade magazine *Marketing Week*, revealed that most people (60 per cent out of a total of 1,492 adults questioned) felt that companies were *'cynically cashing in on public sympathy through cause-related marketing'*. Only weeks after her death, beads were torn from her dresses and sold as earrings at $1,000 a pair. (It is interesting to note that years later, following the tragic events in New York on '9–11', the sales of T-shirts showing the devastated 'ground zero' of the World Trade Center and the slogan 'lest we forget' were considered by many US citizens as 'touching' rather than 'tacky' – a clear example of how market perceptions change according to local perceptions.)

Did you know?

The first product to officially use the Diana logo was Flora margarine. Whilst at the first anniversary of her death over 1,000 products still awaited official Fund approval, it was reported that only 6 per cent of the British public would commemorate the occasion.

Outstanding brand names become enduring cultural icons which are emulated the world over. In Diana's case her 'brand' paraphernalia included the West African Togo Republic selling special edition stamps for the equivalent of two months' salary in that country. Tourist shops sold everything from Diana mugs and spoons, to Diana medals and plates, and so on. Even the Internet drew capital from the rogue Diana industry through a site featuring a computer game based on Diana's fatal road accident with players 'driving' a Mercedes at high speed while being chased by paparazzi on motorbikes.

Which is why any good name worth valuing is also worth protecting. Too many 'extensions' of a brand can actually do more harm than good. You must ask yourself whether it is better to plaster a brand name everywhere, from watches to soap, or protect a valued name, allowing it to be used only in context.

Did you know?
The famous 'Marlboro man' was invented in the 1960s. Originally, the company was British with a shop in Bond Street, London. The name, 'Marlborough' had an aristocratic connotation. In the beginning, the cigarette – then with a red tip, was aimed at women. (*See also*, 'World's greatest brand names', page 162.)

Flying high and proud?

Chris Holt, formerly from British Airways, told me about how and why the airline developed what turned out to be a distinctive corporate branding plan, yet from a marketing viewpoint a touch underwhelming:

> British Airways' branding was meant to be a visual manifestation of the company's personality. It's based on what we referred to as the Masterbrand Repositioning Programme. The project was primarily aimed at defining and, if necessary, repositioning the masterbrand of British Airways.
>
> BA carried out research amongst design professionals in the UK as well as customers around the world. BA set about the task of carrying out a visual audit and visual update in key global places to see to what extent our identity was fit for its present as well as future purpose. Initially, BA approached 50 design consultancies, then

whittled them down to four. The brief was considerably detailed and quite extensive. They all had the same period of time to respond as well as the same sort of funding.

One consultancy at the time, Interbrand Newell and Sorrell, aimed to interpret the airline as being both global and caring in a way appreciated internationally by local communities. This was fundamental to our Masterbrand Repositioning Programme.

Global as well as caring can appear paradoxical in that often the larger the corporation the more impersonal it can seem to potential customers. British Airways operates on a global stage. BA was born and based in Britain, yet dealt with a diverse and rich community of people from all over the world.

Over the centuries, Britain has been an adventurous nation. Particularly in the areas of exploration and world trade. Similarly, instead of being a British airline with global operations, British Airways had become a world airline whose headquarters is in Britain, serving a community of world citizens.

The identity was meant to capture the spirit of a business passionately committed to serving customers and linking diverse communities of the world. The tails on most of the aircraft (excluding Concorde – the flagship) carried versions of specially commissioned works of arts and crafts from communities around the world. The concept was based on the principle that since mankind could make images in the sand, walls or caves, he has created likenesses representing the lifestyle in the community. In other words, British Airways was engaged in the business of bringing people together from all over the world.

Simon Jones, at the time Managing Director of Interbrand Newell and Sorrell, took up the story.

British Airways' concept of world citizenship was visualized through a series of world images commissioned from international artists from different communities. The images are incorporated deeply throughout the airline's brand communications. In this way, rather than being a superficial embodiment of world citizenship within a global community, the brand philosophy enriched every aspect of design from ticketing to signage, check-in desks, baggage labels, in-flight food presentation... in fact, each instance that the public came into contact with the brand.

British Airways unveiled its new corporate image on 10 June 1997. Its previous identity, designed by Landor Associates, dated back to 1984. It featured a harder edged speedwing. The new colours fortified their reputation for safety, security and professionalism – all epitomized in the airline's British roots.

Back to Chris Holt,

> Brand design should reflect both a company's style and personality. It shouldn't be a substitute for it, rather a mirror image. From a branding perspective, there's no point saying one thing in your visual identity and through your advertising, PR and communication if your reality isn't matched.

> In other globalization terms relating to the brand, we discovered that more people are living longer with more disposable income. They travel further for leisure as well as for business purposes. Competition was tougher equally at the expensive, medium and cheaper end of the market. It was vital that British Airways was perceived as being both Global and Caring and thus the first choice airline all around the world.

> By really understanding our customers' requirements, we make our airline appealing. On Japanese routes, we are sensitive to cultural needs, speak Japanese, offer superb Japanese food, provide interesting Japanese in-flight magazines and in-flight entertainment that is not simply subtitled.

Clearly, for British Airways, design played a vital role in their universal branding. It also plays a central role within your imaginative marketing communications mix.

Some of the world's greatest brands. How did they originate?

(All trademarks gratefully acknowledged)

Brand name	Year of origin	Place and origin other details	Founder and/or
Abbey National	1944	Merger between the Abbey Road Building Society (established 1894) and the National Building Society.	
Adidas	1920s	Named after founder of sportswear company. (Umbro are the distributors. Please refer to Umbro below.) In 1997 company acquired French sports company Salomon SA. Now called Adidas–Salomon.	Adolf (Adi) Dassler
Andrex	1945 Changed to Andrex in 1954	Manufactured in St Andrews Road, Walthamstow, London – named after a church. X = excellent or refers teXture.	Merger between Bowater and Scott Paper Company
Aspirin	1899	Derived from Greek by C. Witthauer (scientist) – full name Aceylirte Spirsäure (acetylated spiraeic acid + suffix 'in').	Bayer
Babycham	1949	From, 'baby chamois'.	Francis Showering (of Showering brothers)
Birds Eye	1915	Legend has it that the name referred to ancestral court nobleman named Bird's Eye by a queen after he shot a hawk through the eye with an arrow. Latterly and more commonly accredited to Bob Birdseye, New York based fur trader who originated frozen food process.	Clarence (Bob) Birdseye

Bic	Bic Crystal, introduced to UK 1958	Named after Marcel Bich.	The Bich Brothers, inventors of the disposable pen
Bisto	1910	Possible variation on anagram for Browns, Seasons, Thickens, in One.	Created by RHM Foods
Bovril	First sales 1886–7	Latin 'mix' of Bos, short for bovis = ox and 'vril; from Lord Lytton's novel *The Coming Race*. Bovril AKA Johnston's Fluid Beef. (N.B: 1930s brothels were also known as Bovrils.)	John Lawson Johnston
Brook Bond	1869	Named after tea merchant – Arthur Brook	Alas, no Mr Bond
C&A Modes	1841	Dutch company, initially called Canda (still used) then Cyamodes, then C&A.	Founded by Clemens and August Brenninkmeyer.
Chase Manhattan	1955	Merger between Banks of Manhattan and Chase National Bank of the City of New York.	'Chase' named afer US lawyer and statesman Salmon Portland Chase
Cadbury	1824 First factory 1831	Birmingham	John Cadbury – highly respected Quaker
Coca Cola	1886	Named by the druggist, Dr John S. Pemberton's bookkeeper – Frank Robinson. Based on cola nut and coca leaves. Coca Cola trademark was registered in 1893. John Pemberton sold Coca Cola in 1888 for $2,300. At the time of writing the company is currently worth approximately $18 billion with over 900 million products consumed daily worldwide.	Created by Dr. Pemberton as a brain tonic. First produced in a 3-legged pot in his back-yard. (Following his first ad, only 13 drinks a day for 8 months were sold!)

Dr Martens	1947 – first air-cushioned soles produced. UK production of Dr Martens – 1960	Following a skiing accident (1945) Dr Maertens developed an air-cushioned sole to help to relieve discomfort.	Orthopaedic surgeon, Dr Klaus Maertens and Herbert Flunk – engineer
Disprin	Registered, 1944	Cross between dissolvable and aspirin.	Registered by Roy Vickers of Liverpool
El Al	1948	Established by Israel's first minister of transport. Taken from Hebrew phrase in Hosea 11,7. 'Through them to the most High.'	David Remez
Esso	Origins 1888. Name assumed 1973	Abbreviation of Standard Oil company of New Jersey, set up in 1888. (*Esso* in Italian means 'It' Esso in French means *essence* – petrol.)	Now owned in the UK by Exxon. Originally, S.O co. of New Jersey set up by Rockefeller
Fanta	Second World War	From Fantasie (Developed during the era of Walt Disney's *Fantasia*.)	Coca Cola
Frisbee	1957	From baking tins thrown as a game at Frisbie Bakery, Connecticut.	Fred Morriso
Gillette	Original idea 1895. Production 1903	Dull shaving blades needed expert sharpening, a new method was needed. Razor perfected by William E. Nickerson. (Could this be where the phrase 'nick yourself shaving' derives?)	Idea adapted and enhanced by then Gillette Safety Razor Company.
Gossard	1901. First office 1921. First factory 1926	Undergarments originally inspired by figure of Sarah Bernhardt, actress.	Henry Williamson Gossard
Golden Wonder	1947	Probably inspired by a variety of potato – although it was unsuitable for making chips.	William Alexander

Heinz	1876 (F&J Heinz Company 'F' referred to cousin, Frederick) HJ Heinz Company founded in 1888	Named after Henry Heinz (born 1844). Slogan '57 varieties' inspired by advert on New York railway which read: '21 Styles of Shoes'. Heinz had over 60 products but liked the number, 57.	HJ Heinz – Henry and his brother, John
Hoover	1908	Vacuum cleaner built by J. Murray Spangler. Marketed by William Hoover. (First Hoovers sold for $70.)	William Hoover (British vacuum cleaner invented by H. Cecil Booth)
Hovis	1890 (first in shops)	S Fitton & Son of Macclesfield held a competition to name their bread. A student, Herbert Grimes, won. Name was based on *hominis vis* – Latin = 'the strength of a man/ quantity of men'.	Original flour process was invented by Richard Smith (Smith's Patent Germ Flour)
Imperial Leather	1938	Based on a perfume with the scent of leather (1780s). The perfume was called Eau de Cologne Imperial Leather Russe.	Mr Cusson of Cussons, Sons and Co.
Jaguar	1935	Originally appeared as SS Jaguar (Swallow Sidecar Co. owned by William Lyons). Mr Lyons felt a Jaguar mirrored his car's design and performance. SS was dropped because of the resemblance to the SS Nazi party.	William Lyons
Jell-O	First patented in 1845. Mass produced in 1897	Mary Wait, wife of cough medicine manufacturer, John, invented the term for her spouse's gelatine dessert.	Peal and Mary Wait
Johnson & Johnson	1885	Inspired by the surgeon Sir Joseph Lister who identified airborne germs. Robert, brother of James, Wood Johnson	Robert and James Wood Johnson

		decided to manufacture prepared sterile wrapped surgical dressing. In 1890 in addition to gauze dressings, they sent a tin of Italian talc to a doctor's patient who complained of a skin rash. This was the start of their famous powdered product.	
Kellogg's	1866 – idea 1906 – full production	Wife of Seventh Day Adventist Church minister Dr John Harvey Kellogg suggested a diet to aid 'right living' should be based on foods of vegetable and nut origin. John and brother William, manufactured a toasted flake of maize to replace a heavy breakfast meal (1876). Battle Creek Toasted Corn Flake Company (1906) was founded. To distinguish his brand, William added his signature to each pack.	William Keith and Dr John Harvey Kellogg
Kodak	1888	George Eastman wanted to simplify photography. He developed a camera for the general public. He wrote 'I knew a trade name must be short, vigorous, incapable of being misspelled... The letter K had been a favourite with me... It became a question of trying out a great number of combinations of letters that made words starting and ending with K... Kodak was the result.'	George Eastman
Lego	Introduced as familiar 'brick' in 1950s; previously general wooden toys, 1930s	Ole Kirk Christiansen, a carpenter, made wooden toys. After the Second World War, his son, Gotfred, recognized marketable value from a connectable brick. The rest is history. *Leg godt* in Danish means 'play well'.	Ole Kirk Christiansen

Lucozade	1930s	From glucose and 'ade' – as in cherryade, lemonade. The drink was originally developed by a chemist for his jaundiced daughter. To make it taste sweeter he added orange and lemon oils.	William H. Hunter
Marmite	1920	From French name for stew pot (similar to the shape of the jar). *Oxford Dictionary of Modern English* c.1930s – 'An extract from fresh brewers' yeast, rich in vitamin B complex. Used for culinary purposes, e.g. making soups, etc., and also medicinally.'	Justus Liebig
Mars	c. 1921 Milky Way bar in USA – MARS outside USA.	Franklin C. Mars sold candy from 1902. His son Forrest E. Mars emigrated to the UK in 1932 and introduced the MARS recipe to the English. Originally made by hand, Mars bars sold for 2d each. Milky Way followed in 1935 and then Malteesers.	Franklin C. Mars/Forrest E. Mars
Max Factor	1909	The family business, Max Factor & Co. was formed in 1909, although earlier, Max Fax Snr, a Polish make-up artist opened a perfume, make-up and hair goods concession at the St Louis World's Fair. Son Max created the first make-up for the film industry and then in 1916 broadened his market to the general public.	Max Factor (Jr)
Nescafé	1938	A combination of the manufacturer's name – Nestlé, and the French word for coffee '*café*'	Nestlé (Named after Henri Nestlé) in Vevey, Switzerland
Nabisco	1898 Registered 1901	National Biscuit Company (Acronym)	
Ovaltine	1904	Originally called Ovolmaltine (Latin – *ovum* = egg plus malt, and the suffix, ine	Swiss chemist, Dr George Wander

Oxo	1899	From Ox plus the suffix, o. The product was a refinement of Liebig's (*see* Marmite) 'Extract of Meat'.	
Pepsi Cola	1898	Originally marketed as an elixir to relieve dyspepsia.	Caleb D. Bradham
Persil	1907 Germany 1909 UK	French = 'parsley'. A sprig of parsley was featured as a trade mark by a Frenchman who added bleach to soap. Also: PERborate and SILicate – two ingredients originally included in the product.	Ronchetti
Pretty Polly	1920	Hibbert and Buckland (manufacturers of PP) acquired the name from a wholesaler who originally took the name from a horse called Pretty Polly which had won him a fortune. His daughter told him that the name brought success.	
Quaker Oats	1877	Two versions – you choose! **1** The founder of an American Milling company wanted a name for his product. He chose Quaker from a dictionary as the religious order shared many qualities of oatmeal – strength, honesty, purity, manliness. **2** The founder's partner – William Heston, was inspired by a picture of William Penn, an English Quaker.	Henry D. Seymour William Heston
Racal	1951	Combination of names of partners who founded the company.	Sir Raymond Brown G. Calder Cunningham
Revlon	1932	From the founder of the company who added an L, in honour of one of his partners, Charles Lachman.	Charles Revson (One of their products is called 'Charlie')
Ribena	1930s	Latin botanical name for blackcurrants is *Ribesnigrum*.	H.W. Carter and Co.

Sellotape	1937	Based on a trade name, 'Cellophane' which is the film used in Sellotape.	
Shell	1897... but its roots...	Marcus Samuel had a curio shop in London's East End. His children used to stick sea shells to empty lunch boxes. Each box was named after a resort. He sold the boxes and then offered customers imported, elaborate shell boxes. His shop was known as the Shell Shop. By 1830 he had nurtured an international business in oriental curios. He found a demand for barrelled kerosene at which stage (1897) the international business became Shell Transport and Trading Co. led by his son.	Marcus Samuel
Typhoo	1863	A Birmingham grocer dreamt up the name for his tea because it sounded oriental 'Typhoon' and Tea or Tips made it alliterative.	John Sumner
Toyota	1930s	A Japanese inventor gave his son, who was building a motor car, a patent for an automatic loom designed for a Lancashire weaving company (1929). Being superstitious the family changed the penultimate letter to T since the original TOYODA required ten Japanese letters, TOYOTA only eight which is a lucky number in Japan.	Sakichi Toyoda/ Kiichiro Toyoda
Umbro	1920s	After BROthers Harold and and Wallace HUMphreys (Umbro distributes Adidas, *see* above)	H. Humphreys W. Humphreys
Unilever	1930	From a merger of NV Margarine Unie, Margarine Union and Lever Brothers	William Heskith Lever then Viscount Leverhulme and James Darcy Lever founded the English firm, Lever Brothers

Vauxhall	1903	First car produced in Vauxhall, South London where, in 1857, a Scottish engineer founded the Vauxhall Ironworks.	
Virgin	1970	Name typified the Indie Culture of the 1970s. Plus it entered a relatively 'virgin field' type of approach to business. Richard Branson's first business venture was in 1968 when he published the *Student Magazine*. Virgin Mail order started to operated from 1970 and the first Virgin record shop opened in 1971. Virgin Music Publishing started in 1973. (It is thought that Virgin Records may have alternatively been planned to be called 'Slipped Disc'.)	Richard Branson
Walls	1922	Named after founder whose clerk first suggested the concept of ice-cream in 1913. Wall's brother Fred came up with the idea to sell ice-creams from a tricycle ridden around the streets of West London. 'Stop me and buy one' became one of the twentieth century's most enduring phrases.	Thomas Wall
Wimpy	1954	After the cartoon character Wimpy (featured in Popeye) who adored hamburgers.	
Xerox	Process invented 1937 Xeroxgraphy – popular use 1948	From Greek for 'dry' as xeroxgraphy doesn't use any liquids.	Chester Charlton
Yale	Originally patented 1844 Improved and patented 1861–5 1861–5	After maker – Yale	Linus Yale

10

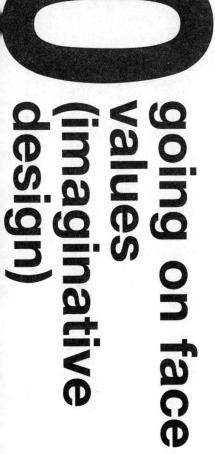

going on face values (imaginative design)

In this chapter you will learn about:

- logos
- typefaces
- colour
- printing
- tribal branding

Good design may quench your inquisitive customers' thirst to try out something which they previously didn't know even existed. Great design includes everything from the mechanisms of a product or service to corporate literature, packaging and even web brand experiences. When carefully implemented, design can also enhance an existing portfolio or fortify your prevailing brand.

Design is the shop window, building fixtures and corporate philosophy of your business all rolled into one. Packaging design outwardly declares your brand, product and service values at the Point of Purchase (POP). Long after your sale has been achieved, packaging on a shelf – like a smartly bound book – continues to speak volumes about your brand and its potentials.

Carefully branded packaging has become an essential marketing tool. In the 1960s when consumers traditionally had more time to linger at supermarket shelves, they would examine each package carefully before making a purchase – so the packaging didn't have to work as hard as it does today.

With less time on everyone's hands, packaging has to convey in milliseconds your brand's total concept. This requires the appropriate use of shape, size, colour, texture and style. These Perceivable Branding Properties (PBPs) unify to make an immediate comforting brand impact which reaches deeply into the subconscious (see also 'Thinking deeper' page 95).

Although humble, one of first impressions you get of a company is its business card. It tells you about the kind of company and the person's status. In designing the business card it is important to provide a clear understanding of that status. In this way, rather than just being seen as a façade, the values of identity are adopted throughout the company and communicated to current and prospective clientele.

Your business card is just the first step to communicating through design – your company's approach, outlook, values and much more (and you thought it was just another card for your roladex!). In highlighting your brand's visually communicated features, even the most modest design modifications help distinguish your brand from your competitors' (D&B – Different & Better).

The house of Marketing – better built by design

In marketing, there are supporting girders of design procedures.

Fashion design. As part of the wider sales promotions' in-store theatre – from the shape of a package to free-gift promotion, wider fashion design embraces clothing, textiles, furniture and car bodies. In the case of clothing, brands may battle for sponsorship space on sporting garments. In catering, again as part of promotional theatre, restaurants often have employees literally wear designs to reflect more than just service on a plate, but with a smile.

Design organization. Rather than being the sole custodian for your design – and concealing its values from the market, aim to be a design *champion*. (Marketers refer to taking responsibility for a brand as brand stewardship.) If not, what starts as a marketing design masterpiece can end up as a colour-by-numbers exercise with each department arguing over who gets to paint which section. (*See also* 'Ten motives for ideological assassination', page 137). Just as the girders provide support to your overall marketing design structure, so areas of design expertise construct walls embellished with colour and shade.

Graphic design includes corporate identity, television and video titling and form as well as packaging and styling – including brochures, magazines and web design.

Interior design provides visual as well as tactile substance to exhibition stands, events, shops, offices and buildings including special marketing-led structures. (Gillian Thomas, former Director of the Children's Gallery of The Science Museum, in London, is accredited to have said '*By altering the graphic content of an exhibit you could double the number of people who visited it*'.)

During the 1980s, architecture was big, bold and brash, especially commissioned by conglomerates who proudly displayed their wealth peacock-like. Today, successful companies still build big, but not necessarily bold. Many design vast interior open spaces – especially at entrances and receptions. This mimicry of the great outdoors often extends to planting trees indoors (presumably driving a marketing message of openness and confidence to both employees and customers). It is also further indicative of working in a networked age where people can move seating arrangements around different parts of the company – quiet areas, busy areas and so on – all helping to stimulate imaginative thinking.

The barbershop pole syndrome

For smaller outlets such as confectioners, hairdressers, restaurants, dry cleaners... it pays to expand a corporate identity programme (featuring all your imaginative marketing values) to the shop front. Your presence on the high street isn't merely acknowledged, but made exceptional. For example, traditionally, men's hairdressers featured barbershop columns with revolving red spirals outside their establishments. On the upside, the public immediately recognized the service provided. However, this drawing together of barbers into one hair-crops of 'me toos' didn't add any real personality or value to the individual proprietor. By becoming distinctive you gain the edge over competitive retailers. Then, given a choice based on your total image, the shopper visits your store first. (Designers call this, '*taking ownership*' of your identity).

Product design works hand in glove with the marketing process. By considering what is marketable for a specific type of audience, a product designer can adapt designs accordingly. The more time invested in perfecting the design of your product, the less is the marketing budget needed to convince the public that they need it. The Design Innovation Group of The Open University in the UK is quoted by the Design Council as saying, '*90 per cent of new product developments which use a professional design consultant make profits and the average pay-back period is just 15 months*'.

Fashion and textile. This is one of the most powerful mediums for communicating a marketing message. (*See* 'Product Life Cycle' page 18.)

Making your mark

Chris Holt, formerly from British Airways earlier noted, '*mankind has long created images in the sand, walls or caves*'. Today those images have become icons which instantly communicate a brand's value. In many instances, if we want to get more information about something, rather than read about it we'll get the general picture on television then detail from newspapers, radio and of course the web.

Company logos combine appropriate image, colours, typeface and size in a visually arresting statement. As products become more alike and competitive, so design makes those products individually attractive.

Your logo mirrors your marketing values. As your company slowly evolves, so your logo may alter slightly over the years until you reach a period of major political or social change – often around ten years. Then it's time to refine the logo dramatically. I have divided logos into six distinctive categories:

1 Light-hearted logos reflecting a fresh, youthful approach to business.
2 Plain and simple. Just a typeface logo or style of type on a coloured background (usually shaded with the typeface 'reversed out'). It doesn't commit the company to one image or another but conveys efficiency and professionalism.
3 Illustrations representing the kind of service the company provides. (e.g. fits double glazing – so a picture of a window, or serves hamburgers – picture of burger).
4 Key letters from a company or a combination of a merged organization. This 'back to basics' approach works if your company doesn't dare take risks with perceptions (many financial institutions opt for this approach).
5 Abstract shapes, which appear to be hand finished, (giving a personal touch). Examples include abstract designs – often featured by 'trendy' organizations.
6 Logos featuring a founder's signature.

Your logo type should have its own personality. Once the shape, texture and applications of that imagery have been finalized, you should nurture and keep a logo faithful to your corporate values. Aggressively diluting your image, like irrationally over-stretching your brand name, can lead to confusion and, ultimately, disaster. Family brands, too, have to share some degree of fidelity with the core brand design.

As with the example of Nike, simple, dynamic logos are not simply seen, but taken to consumers' hearts.

Usually, to arrive at a final logo, you have to consider scores of choices – often within focus-group settings. John Harris, design consultant to Creative Interpartners, explains

It's not just painting the face of a company simply for the sake of it – that's too cosmetic. It's making visible by design, the strategy and aspirations of a company. In this way, what is being perceived on the inside of an organization is in line with an external audience's perception.

If you accept that people tend to judge books initially by their jacket rather than take time to glance through their contents, you'll also appreciate why it is important that your logo should be seen as more than just another official mark. John Harris remarks further:

> When you design a logo, you are reflecting the personality of an organization. You are peering into the very spirit of an organisation and sharing those virtues with a target audience. In this way, an identity is embraced and warmly appreciated as an accessible, relevant icon rather than an inaccessible, aloof corporate figure head.

the creativity works
www.theworks.co.uk

A marketing logo for the twenty-first century

The company logo, above, had to be:

- accessible
- creative
- distinctive
- representative of a planned, strategic approach to creativity
- comprehensible in any language
- contemporary
- fun and adaptable – allowing the smaller figure to assume different roles for future service extensions and developments
- supported at its foundation by a professional, visually strong, company title
- representative of a problem-solving, pro-active attitude
- By soft brush stroking the character, the personality becomes especially appealing, encouraging the sense of a hands-on approach to business.

Just your type

Every company is absorbed in paperwork. The structuring of forms is another medium of making design responsible to your overall value-added objectives. Organized forms don't merely feature a company badge on every page. (Originally, in the

United States, branding was practised by cowboys who 'branded' herds as if badging them.) The style forms should also reflect the company's philosophy towards ideals such as simplicity and professionalism.

Typefaces (collectively known as fonts) provide a further clue to your style and type of company. From **bold** to *italic* to CAPITALS and Upper and Lower Caps, the form of your typeface hints at the character of your business. The important thing to keep in mind when choosing a typeface is that the style and format of the type on a page or even Internet site, must never obscure your overall message.

There are literally thousands of type designs. You can even buy a computer program contriving a typeface based on your handwriting.

Did you know?
The standard typesetting unit was first proposed by the eighteenth-century French typographer Pierre Fournier. He called it the 'point'. It was developed by Firmin Didot into today's European standard. Until metric measures were universally adopted, standard sizes differed slightly from Anglo-American versions.

Kerning reduces the space between letters. This technique is often used by publishers to accommodate words on a page. Professional typographers adjust lettering, so enabling words to create an even pattern.

For example, if you type the word **L APTOP**, you sometimes get an awkward shape. However, add kerning and, as if by magic, you arrive at a more comfortable and so balanced word – **LAPTOP**.

Leading originally referred to the lead used to separate lines of text by printing houses. Leaded type is therefore set with leads between the lines. This is because correct leading makes body copy more legible.

Paint me a vision (The use of colour in logos)

Colour doesn't simply make you *look* different but it makes you and, more importantly, those with whom you come into contact, *feel* different.

Vivid colours alert

Pastel colours pacify

Unusual sizes and shapes attract interest

Contrasting shades
stimulate

Traditionally, the more 'professional' the company, the more non-partisan the colours. During the 1990s, businesses heavily featured grey or steel colours. Today, companies tend to opt for either vibrant colours like blue on yellow, or more pastel backgrounds, reflecting a gentler yet quietly confident image. It is vital that, when thinking about a colour for inclusion within your identity, that, like corporate designs in general, you don't simply mix and match elements from other companies. Your design must be as individual as your company. The idea is to convey your values rather than hijack someone else's.

Below are suggested colour types for logos (based on a selection of typical logo types).

Type of product/service	Typical colour
Confident, cool, sincere and fresh Creative, solution provider (One of the most popular options. Works well with complementary colours, especially yellow.)	Light blue
Fresh produce, environmental goods, get-up-and-go products – like invigorating bath oils. (In the Middle East, green often equates to religious symbolism.)	Green
Communication – harmony, design, sales, television/entertainment providers	Yellow
Community or sensual	Peach/pink/ apricot
Fast food, Internet gaming, investments	Purple/maroon

Active, such as sporting, discos, clubs	Red
Educational, executive professions	Royal or dark blue
Religious, welfare	Mauve/dark red
Essential, highly practical business services	Brown
Higher market financial services	Gold
Personal, tailor-made services	Silver
One-off services or discreet products	Pale grey/white
'No-nonsense' services – law enforcement, or any authoritative figure. Works well contrasted against vivid, colours such as orange.	Black

Web logos

If you plan to animate your logo on the web, do so cautiously. Animation for its own sake will never convey the total 'feel' for your company. Go through the same design auditing process as on printed material – ensuring your values are reflected in every detail of your website's layout.

Colour to your ears (Audio logos)

One other kind is the sound logo. This is the sign-off used on radio commercials where, obviously, print is impractical. Jingles can be as colourful and intricate as a printed design so should be produced accordingly. (More details are in *Teach Yourself Copywriting* – (*see* 'Taking it Further').

Did you know?
Many logos feature wildlife (Esso is an example). You can imaginatively capitalize upon this by donating some of your profits to the chosen animal's wildlife fund. This shows you care as much for your environment as your image.

It looks great on paper

Printing *can* be an expensive business. It needn't be. There are ways to cheat the colour process. The most commonly used method is to print a tint of the full colour. Just use your corporate colour and a tint of it (provided you don't feature too many tints as it can look a total mess!). This said, I believe that design is too important to cheat on colour, just for the sake of saving a few pennies here and there.

Another thing to bear in mind is to consider how your colour(s) reproduce on different formats. Check with your printer to see how it looks on standard letter headed paper and on laser copy paper. You'll be amazed by the difference. Also ask to see how it reproduces on a business card. Finally, consider how it will reproduce on the side of delivery vans, on stickers, boxes, labels, signs, forms, clothing, exhibition boards, advertisements, and so on.

Eight deadly printing sins

1 Over/under printing quantities.
2 Printing on the wrong material. (Always keep a box full of samples – and ask to see more. Many pay a high price when they attempt to be *too clever* with paper sizes and weights.)
3 Overlooking how print is finished – do you want it laminated, stitched, folded...?
4 Assuming any photograph can be reproduced simply.
5 Not budgeting for proofs.
6 Under-estimating print/delivery times.
7 Not checking mailing restrictions if posting business reply coupons.
8 Opting for the first quote that comes through the door.

Perfectly packaged communication

Packaging is the tactile manifestation of your brand. It gives your product substance. It imbues independence and instils confidence. Logos and other printed corporate identity provide a sense of feeling for a brand. Like love at first sight, packaging takes those emotions on to the next stage in a relationship. It is the sensuous moment, when your customers reach out, hold and experience the feel, texture and shape of a marketing 'promise' for themselves.

A classic example of packaging is the Coca Cola bottle. The original straight-sided bottle design was introduced around 1910. By 1915, the company needed a distinctive corporate identity. It is thought that the familiar curvaceous bottle was based on one of the drink's main ingredients – the cola nut. Around the time, *Life* magazine featured an article about the bottle which said of the packaging... '*It remains the queen of the soft drink container... Its shape is aggressively female – a quality that, in merchandise as in life, sometimes transcends functionalism.*'

Together with Coca Cola's dynamic contour curve introduced in 1970, today's Coke is one of the most recognized symbols on the planet.

> **Marketing in action**
> The grandfather of Lana Turner (the 1940s Hollywood star) invested in Coca Cola. But he didn't think the name would ever catch on. So he withdrew his investment and instead chose what he felt would be a much shrewder option – The Raspberry Cola Company.

Perfume companies have long recognized that the sweet aroma of success depends, to a large extent, on the style and design of the container. Similarly, alcoholic drink companies invest as much time in perfecting the shape of a bottle as balancing the flavours. The style of that packaging, like all aspects of great design, is interpreted throughout their marketing communications.

This was illustrated when an executive of an alcoholic brand confided in me that, except for the addition of fruit juice flavourings, many alcoholic drinks aimed at the young were designed to be virtually tasteless. After all, he explained, youngsters want to drink as much as possible without a lingering bitter taste in their mouths. Thus, whilst there may not be that taste *inside* the bottle, the *outer* shell tells another story. Go along to any trendy night club and you'll see fashionable drinkers – especially men, clasping bottles of designer beer and lager to their chests. It's as if they are visually 'saying' '*love me, love my choice of brand.*'

I call this clique-specific marketing Tribal Branding. It hearkens back to when we lived in caves, hunted in groups and based ideals on peers. (*See also*, 'The evolution of marketing', page 3.)

This packaging philosophy is also practised in retail outlets. For example, many consumers will buy clothes not just because of how comfortably they fit but because they are attracted to the lifestyle depicted on the packaging, even extending to graphics on in-store posters. Lifestyle marketing as a concept explains the feeling and what can't be sensed by words alone.

Another element of responsible design is the training of your teams who provide a service. Here, the importance of business grooming and developing your people within the service sector assumes equal ranking to the way you package manufactured goods.

Nothing to be sniffed at

An up-and-coming stratagem takes imaginative design into a new dimension beyond sight, sound and touch. Smell is one of the most provocative of all sensations. A scent can remind you of a holiday or childhood. Just like a holiday memory often relates to lazy summer days, so smells have their seasons. Rich, spicy smells like mulled wine have winter flavours perhaps suitable for marketing woollen clothing. Floral fragrances and citrus bouquets are worth considering for marketing fresh environmental products.

Charities for the blind have been known to successfully impregnate their mailings with scent. Pass by a coffee shop brewing freshly ground coffee and the temptation to treat yourself to a cup of coffee becomes virtually irresistible. Fresh bread can have a similar effect.

Too much of a smell can put off prospective buyers. Too little and you irritate as they try to pinpoint the aroma's source. Some airlines have corporate scents. They subtly pump the smell of fresh leather into the first-class cabin. Others develop a certain sweet perfume which captures the freshness and vitality of a service. This technique can also be adapted by long-haul coach operators to keep passengers relaxed and sickness-free, or night clubs which prefer that customers smell invigorating aromas rather than sweat!

If you venture into the area of odour marketing, do so at your peril. For heavenly smell is in the nose of the beholder. Remember, take responsibility for your design at every level of implementation and you can secure the lead within your sector.

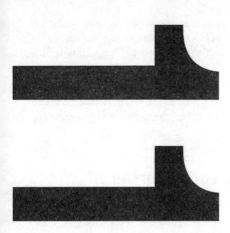

generating demand

In this chapter you will learn about:
- written and personal presentations
- structuring your marketing talk
- tips for better presentations

At some point, unless selling via the Internet (not using digital cameras), direct mail or non-3G enabled telephone, you have to come face to face with prospective consumers. This can sound a frightening experience (no reflection on any of your current charming customers!). However, it needn't be so.

Apart from end-of-year budgeting, one of the things that can make marketers really nervous is making a presentation either on paper or in person.

Written sales and other forms of presentation

Let's deal first with being effective on paper. As a lecturer, I am often asked by marketers how to prepare successful reports.

Reports come in two main flavours – information and proposals. A common mistake is getting an informative report mixed up with a proposal.

Typically, a report acquaints the reader with such aspects as the history of a product or service and current state of play – including information on marketing projects and on the various departments within the organization. On the other hand, a proposal needs to be supported by realism and objectivity. Unlike writing a report, a proposal allows for added imaginative insights. This includes predicting events and opportunities and hopefully persuading the reader to do something – if only to act as an advocate on your behalf.

Just as proposals sway opinions, so there are four stages leading to each successful implementation.

1 The *scenario* – recognizing the overall situation in which the reader (hopefully) feels a degree of allegiance.
2 The *enigma* – highlighting the immediate needs to be resolved before addressing a wider picture.
3 The *options* available.
4 The *recommended course of action* – following assessment of all logical alternatives.

Each stage should be supported by arguments leading to a conclusive recommendation. Additional support – graphs, enclosures, and so forth, should be recorded in the appendix. Then, the main thrust of the argument is not clouded.

This technique works well in any proposal format (including detailed emails). All proposals should be directed to the reader as distinct from the organization. It's only through demonstrating how you can satisfy a prospect's needs that you can automatically demonstrate your organization's ability to deliver appropriate proposals. Above all, remember that both reports and proposals are really means to a practical solution.

Personal presentations

Being eloquent on paper is one thing – being persuasive as a speaker is another. Even the simplest of personal presentations – speeches at weddings – can be a nightmare, both to the speaker and the defenceless audience.

When making a personal address, the speaker's main goal should be to leave a lasting and realistic impression with the audience.

The greater your own knowledge and understanding of the audience, the more pertinent and personal your speech. When preparing a marketing speech, before writing a word, keep cross-referring in your mind how it will benefit the assembly. Consider their situation, interests, ambitions, possible objections, and so on. Also, think about your props such as overheads, laptops, and so on. If using multimedia, you could experiment in setting the screen type size to no less than 22pt, in white or yellow, highlighted against a mellow background – such as blue.

As with presenting your ideas on paper, there are two types of oral presentation technique.

The *informative* approach depicts, defines, demonstrates and corroborates. (Defining issues is a great way to start an informative marketing speech. For example, 'Marketing – according to the Chartered Institute of Marketing it means...'

The *influential* approach appeals to passions tempered by reasoning and logic. Here the aim is to incite action or inspire belief.

Did you know?
If you are stuck for a title for your speech, try names from famous records or titles from classic books.

You've finished what you want to say, but are you still talking?

Marketing speeches take longer to plan than to write. Try not to speak for more than 20 minutes. This equates to 2,000 words, allowing you to pace your talk comfortably to 100 words per minute. If you are a novice at delivering marketing speeches, why not try writing the speech in its entirety? The downside of reading a speech is that it can sound staccato. Worse still, you may lose your place. You can avoid both hurdles by rehearsing either to a mirror or to colleagues, typing the script with double-line spacing and underlining key words or sentences which help you to keep track as well as emphasize points.

Index cards can be helpful if you want to improvise on key points – one per card, as you go along, However, if this kind of speech delivery is new to you, be careful not to ramble on too much.

Once you have outlined your speech, you need to add substance. It's this substance that provides insight and credibility to what you have to say. Below are two popular marketing-speech delivery structures.

Step by step
This is the basic method, whereby you state a problem then follow with the issues caused by the problem (or situation) and then conclude with a solution.

Inspector Morse
State the obvious – '*Teach Yourself Marketing explains invaluable marketing techniques*'. Then carry out a little detective work on your statement: '*This book is crammed with career-boosting tips.*' Therefore '*reading this book will provide you with techniques to enhance your marketing career.*' (*See also* Aristotle, page 131.)

Speech structure

Section	Possible 'hooks'
Intro (establish rapport	*Ask a question.* If to a small audience – directly – allowing for no more than two answers – if any. Better still, rhetorically.
and credibility)	*Refer to a date and its significance.* Show key statistics and describe why and how they are relevant.
	Tell a joke. Avoid it unless you are a raconteur.
	Relate to a piece of news or recent event.
	Quote someone famous. Only if your interpretation of the quote is of greater relevance than the original quote (e.g. in a marketing speech to the agricultural community: 'George Orwell said: "advertising is the rattling of a stick inside a swill bucket". I say that's great if you're advertising buckets to pig farmers.'
Body (convey reasoning)	Overview what has occurred. Where do you currently stand and where could you go? (This is particularly effective if you want to put across a new marketing direction.)
	Interpret a situation. Explain what it is, what it does, how it directly affects the audience, where it's going and why they should care.
	Bust a scandal. Often used if your organization suffers a public relations disaster or is subject to malicious industry gossip. • Face the accusation head on, describing it in full – no holds barred. • Counter the rumour or accusation with hard facts – not hearsay.
	(In all marketing speeches, try to avoid personality politics. Exclude phrases like, 'I think' or 'My view is'.

Feel it.

Selectively repeat a key word to re-enforce an objective, (e.g. *IF* it were better, *IF* it were clear. *IF* we went further…)

Other typical power phrases include:

- Read my lips…
- No pain, no gain
- Don't ask why… Demand why not…
- We haven't even started, yet; we're at the start of a new era.
- Can you see what I feel?
- Never again
- I rather run towards an opportunity now, than run away from a disaster later.
- We need to offer marketing jobs – not promises. I promise jobs not just marketing offers.

Close (hammer home the message)	*Reverse mapping.* That is where we were; this is how I recommend where we want to be. It's down to you to take up the gauntlet.

Things to watch

- Arrive on time.
- Never criticize your audience.
- Don't skip slide details.
- Allow time for questions and answers.
- Avoid UFOs – Un Funny Observations.
- Practise and be familiar with your slides.
- Spell-check your slides.
- Switch off mobile phones.
- Look confident. Think confidently.
- Don't apologize for your presentation or lack of preparation.
- Don't talk to one person – address the entire audience personally – embellishing your talk with relevant anecdotes.
- Don't keep looking at your wrist watch.
- Pre-check that everything works/carry a spare plug and be ready to talk unaided by slides.

Marketing in action

Debate the following with your colleagues: The art of public oration is dead. Then deliver a five-minute speech supporting your point of view.

12

some inspire naturally, the rest use a pr consultant

In this chapter you will learn about:
- key pr indicators
- news or propaganda?
- charity pr
- pr and sponsorship
- events and pr

Public relations (PR) is an essential part of your communications mix. It provides a strong voice in a sea of noise where crowded advertising dilutes your message – the clutter effect. It generates awareness, creates need and influences decision makers. Effectively implemented, PR builds bridges of understanding between you and all who deal with you.

PR is not simply a matter of dealing with the press. Every aspect of relationship-building is touched by PR: from encouraging and cajoling investors at special events and via newsletters to working with the local community, lobbying parliament or launching a new trade marketing initiative. In this way, PR addresses general perceptions of an organization through its public persona as well as through direct personal relationships. Which is why PR plays such a vital role within your total marketing relationships programme. It is important to use PR to expose a specific business issue, rather than be manipulated by the press to expose your personal life. Whenever in doubt, revert to the standard politician's response to difficult questions – answer a more '*appropriate*' one instead.

Be the ring leader in the Media Circus

To be memorable – for the right reasons! – imaginative PR should:

- Be cost effective – Typically, PR accounts for around 10 per cent of your marketing budget. Just as there is no free advertising, so there are no free PR lunches – even with members of the press. PR takes time, a labour resource and, therefore, money.
- PR should be directed at specific audiences via well-known channels. (*See also* 'Watching the detectives', page 90).
- At all times, PR must be honest.
- What do you want to achieve? (e.g. influence, alter conceptions, develop alliances.)
- Consider where your publicity appears. If in print, then your comments should be in-depth. The glossier the print, the longer the magazine's reading life, so the more that your comments can be scrutinized.
- If television, appearances take precedent over profundity of comment.
- If radio, be prepared to squeeze into seconds what, unless a dramatic story, may only be remembered for minutes.
- Your message should be tactically clear (short term) and strategically consistent (long term).

From PRessure to pleasure

You can gauge public perceptions through opinion polls or press coverage. (Without company stories, the trade press in particular would have little news to report.) Try to plan where you would like your story to appear. Could it be a main news-grabbing article, in-depth feature or perhaps hidden elsewhere as a 'filler'?

Key PR indicators

Television Rating points (TVR) – Each TVR compares to reaching 1 per cent of the population using a 30-second commercial.

Opportunities To See (OTS) – The number of occasions that your item is seen.

Gross Rating Points (GRP) – The total number of people reached by a medium at one time. (One GPR is the equivalent of 1 per cent of the population.)

Compare your PR communication channels. Was a Business Briefing Breakfast with key influencers more valuable than say, sending a press release? What feedback did you get from publicity on the Internet? Have you earned media respect? Which medium delivers best results, advertising or PR? Draw on the parts rather than sum total of your efforts. Exploit and make PR work even harder for you.

Weighing up the truth

In the United States, you can sue if you are misrepresented. In the United Kingdom, if you want to 'take a company to the cleaners' one of your first options is to approach the press. Familiarize yourself with the Economy of Truth scale. Depending on how much you wish to reveal or defend, your position on the scale alters. Anything approaching the absolute line of truth needs serious consideration. Anything below this point should be avoided at all costs.

Economy of truth scale

PR opportunities

In *Teach Yourself Copywriting* (*see* 'Taking it Further'), I discuss composing a press release. But there is more to handling news than writing for the external media, including newsletters.

News or propaganda?

Concerning newsletters – are you writing about news or promoting sales? If it is purely the latter, then it shouldn't be called a newsletter but something like a sales update, bulletin or sales letter. If it is none of these sales variations, you should consider the newsletter's style and format. Here, design, again, plays a key role. A badly produced/designed newsletter adds no substance to your organization's marketing values.

Types of newsletter

Standard A3, folded down to A4 flyer. Used as an updating device rather than a substantial magazine discussion format.

Poster newsletter. Up to A2 size which is a cross between a general information board and a promotional poster pinned to company notice boards, such as in the coffee room.

Newssheet. Follows the same standards as a traditional newspaper format. This includes sections for different parts of your organization as well as reports or stories. Just as newspaper stories are listed in terms of newsworthiness starting from the front and back and working towards the centre, so there should be space allocated for more trivial pursuits such as crosswords, births, deaths and retirement as well as social matters. As with all newsletters, it is essential that you are sure of your audience type. Just because Mary in Accounts is pregnant, that may not be 'newsworthy' to customers – unless, of course, one of them is responsible!

E-news letters. Published on the Internet or company Intranet. They offer scope for instant updates and feedback.

Company magazine. A fast growing sector of corporate news and brand lifestyle communication. Contract magazine publishing covers everything from pop music fanzines to in-store magazines and glossy lifestyle publications. All enhance customer care, thereby loyalty, through making individuals feel valued. Some include tailored sections which address individual interests such as skiing supplements for trendy winter sports seekers or antiques supplements for discerning investors.

Four things to communicate other than news in a newsletter

1 Encourage sales – including cross selling.
2 Increase awareness.
3 Promote a sense of a company's character.
4 Act as a research vehicle.

Hold the front page

A good newsletter story is divided into components:

• The headline – captures the subject's spirit and account.
• The lead – picks up the relevant issues.
• The body – details those issues.

- The support – draws on expert opinion and public reaction.
- The conclusion – summarizes the findings.

Adding star quality

Aligning your brand with a celebrity often pays large dividends – provided the celebrity is suitable and cost effective. NOP research revealed that 62 per cent of 15–24 year olds agreed that ads were particularly appealing if they featured a celebrity.

At the other end of the sponsorship age spectrum, Castrol Oil, Budweiser and Volkswagen have kept the bands like Rolling Stones rolling. It's all a question of appropriate markets for your brand.

Did you know?

A 'classic' marketing cautionary tale relating to pop bands involves Geri Halliwell formerly 'Ginger' Spice who left the Spice Girls and their sponsors with a potential dilemma when she decided to leave the band, especially as some sponsors like Sony had invested in a software game called Spice World. Walkers Crisps featured the first picture of the remaining four spice girls after the break up and used it as part of their promotion to launch a children's snack food called 'Cheetos'.

Did you know?

In the UK, the first alcohol brand to sponsor a series on morning television was Martini Citro. Made in Italy, the series was presented by an Italian chef and chosen to reflect the brand's target core market: 25–34-year-old women.

Charity sponsorship

I wrote a book called *The Meaning of Life*, proceeds of which went to the British Red Cross. I am indebted to them for the following top ten celebrity tips.

Tips for charities involving celebrities

1 Ensure the celebrity is well briefed and made to feel important.
2 A personality should be looked after throughout and kept happy at all times.

3 Pay basic expenses. Send a car or forward a cheque if they are driving themselves, send train tickets, or pay for air fares if they are on an overseas visit.

4 'Thank yous' are important. Birthday cards, flowers, get well cards, short notes and telephone calls are significant, too.

5 Sometimes invite celebrities to important functions without asking them to do anything! Just their presence at an annual meeting, at a celebration party, or even just to see work is appreciated.

6 Involve celebrities in the planning decisions. Ask what they would like to do. They must not feel that they are being given orders. Their knowledge of fund-raising and publicity opportunities is a great asset.

7 Keep on the right side of secretaries, personal assistants, or celebrities' spouses. Celebrities rarely manage their own diaries. If you need a favour, consult assistants whose support is vital.

8 Monitor the media for anything that may affect your celebrity supporters. If they have received an honour or suffered a sad loss, appropriate letters are important.

9 Don't worry about public opinion concerning whether today's celebrity may be tomorrow's has-been. They may make a 'comeback,' and contribute a valuable endorsement. Besides, how will other celebrities feel if they see you drop a contemporary like a hot potato?

10 Above all, treat celebrities as your best friends.

Marketing in action

There's another drought in Africa. Yet although up to 1 million may perish, the public is apathetic towards charitable appeals. Should you consider launching an emergency lottery-ticket promotion or should you use a high-profile celebrity to highlight your cause? Why?

A word from our sponsors

You can sponsor anything from your local school team to cricket club or a special event. It shows that your organization shares the values of spectators/participants and is part of, and cares for, the community. By doing so, your brand improves image, integrity and name recall value. This generates a sponsorship aurora where consumer sensitivity is shifted on to your brand.

Did you know?
On first glance, readers spend less than half a second looking at each component (e.g. headline and picture) which makes up an ad.

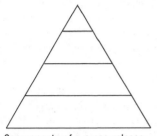

Headline – eye catcher

First paragraph – 'guts' of your story – short and to the point

Support details

Source, quotes, etc.

Components of a press release

NB: Try, whenever possible to align your story with a wider news event. Also, call journalists on the phone and 'pitch' the merits of your story, followed by sending out the release, which can be archived on your website.

A highly controversial sponsorship concerns sports and smoking. Tobacco companies argue that they wish only to encourage existing smokers to switch brands, rather than recruit new smokers – 30 per cent of UK smokers change brands every year. The companies further maintain that children smoke because of peer pressure, siblings and parents who already smoke. However, in India for example, a study showed that children who saw a particular cigarette brand throughout a soccer World Cup event, concluded that smoking improves playing!

Similarly, classroom sponsorship can be 'tricky'. You can sponsor textbooks and feature in-school posters. Additionally, you can 'badge' equipment with your logo – such as on computers. Appropriately marketed, your company will be appreciated for improving standards of education rather than image.

In the United States, drinks companies battle for exclusive rights to have their vending machines in schools. Marketers have long recognized the playground currency of Pester Power, that is when children harass parents to buy a product. However, children are 'advertising aware', never to be under-estimated in their power to 'filter' messages. Act responsibly and your integrity will return handsome dividends.

Make an impression – not an exhibit of yourself

Successful exhibitions depend on planning as far ahead as a year before the event. Check your budget, space allocation and anticipated appropriate attendance.

At least six months prior to the event, ensure you have the materials for your set – either kit form or bespoke, as well as uniforms, give aways and so on. Also pre-book any overnight accommodation. When designing your set, keep in mind your brand image as well as the overall theme of the show. Stands should be 'open' with maximum access to visitors. Keep copywriting on your display boards to a minimum, the objective of all displays being to explain who you are, what you do and why you do it better. If you use video, make sure the programme is subtitled, short – no more than three minutes – and continuously looped. If exhibiting abroad, double check aspects like height of rooms (so your set fits in) and power points (so it all works).

Did you know?
Reserve your stand near the dining area. You'll significantly increase visitor traffic. More if it's also near the toilets. Additionally, security guards often converge in the restaurant area. If this is opposite to your stand, you'll have extra security at no cost (people pilfer from stands).

Three months – Prepare pre-event publicity such as advertising, direct-mail invitations and press releases. Also a good time to arrange special client hospitality, reservations at local restaurants, and so on.

Six weeks – Brief staff. Re-check all your materials, including stock of business cards, brochures, display units, order pads, and so forth. (At the event, make sure you distribute your brochures to the on-site press office.)

Three to two weeks – Send reminder invitations to key prospects and guests.

One week before – Check documentation (including credit cards and passports if travelling overseas).

The day before – It's all panic stations! Anticipate things not being properly connected, flooring unlaid, extra flowers needed to hide wiring... Provided you are prepared, you'll take it all in your stride.

At the show – RELAX. Let the event work for you. People attend to pick up information and network. For your part, meet and greet visitors with open-ended questions *not 'Can I help you?' – the answer is usually –* 'No'. Find time to chat with other exhibitors.

Following the show – Distribute sales leads (followed up within ten days – leads cool by about 12 per cent every three days), thank everyone who helped make the event a success and learn for next time.

Marketing in action

Referring to the newsletter story format formula, devise a story about your latest trade fair event.

13

direct response – from junk mail to jump marketing

In this chapter you will learn about:
- listing services
- direct mail targeting
- integrated marketing

Direct marketing – sometimes called integrated, quantitative, one-to-one, database, relationship or through-the-line marketing – measures success by response. Used imaginatively, it supports your brand values as well as tactical objectives. As discussed previously and contrary to popular belief, direct marketing is not solely concerned with direct mail. It encompasses the full gambit of the communications mix including loose inserts, advertisements, radio commercials, direct response television and the Internet.

Whichever medium is chosen, by being personal, direct marketing makes your communication relevant, clear, intriguing (illustrating the key benefits of a product or service) ... and so establishes the basis for a dialogue. Like meeting people for the first time, the better pre-informed you are, the more is likely to be gained from the developing relationship.

Searching for clues

From a sales perspective, the whole world is your oyster. But valuable pearls are rare. If your direct marketing lands in the wrong hands, irrespective of its content or design, it's a waste of money and your efforts have simply produced junk mail. What's needed is a communication that makes a prospect jump up and pay attention to what you have to say. This is where profiling enters into the scenario.

What irritates people most?

When it comes to consumer direct mailing, be wary of excessive prize-draw rules, misleading propositions and unsubstantiated claims. (If you do run a prize draw, remember that participants are never obligated to enter into a purchase.)

Your aim is to match prospects with existing customers. Commercial listings include consumer based information – such as where people live, what they enjoy and so on, to business listings which segment according to job titles, geographic areas, types of companies. Additonally, you can target directors at home, Small Office, Home Office businesses and members of trade organizations.

Comprehensive consumer lists include: postcode data available as software for simple identification of an entire address by house number alone (ideal for telemarketing); geodemographic classifications; subscriptions to magazines; lifestyle club membership; propensity to donate to a charity; credit card

Junk Mail	65%
Drivers hogging the middle lane of the motorway	34%
Companies where phone is answered by a recorded message	33%
People using mobile phones in public places	29%
Car/house alarms going off	29%
Too few checkouts at the supermarket	24%
Piped music	17%
Plastic shopping bags that split	13%
Traffic lights that turn red at pedestrian-free crossings	13%
Opening Tetrapack cartons	11%
Programming video recorders	4%
Hand dryers in public toilets	4%

Source: NOP. Respondents answered at least 3 questions from a list of 12.

ownership – the list is forever growing. Make sure your list is 'clean', in other words, up to date with no 'gone-aways' or deaths. 2003 Royal Mail research pointed to UK small businesses losing over £3bn a year through poor communication. You can often negotiate net name agreement discounts for names which have been disregarded after cleaning against other lists as well as through profiling.

Did you know?
To increase awareness of postcodes, the UK Post Office once promoted a quiz featuring just one question – *What's your postcode?* Only a few responses were received – it was discovered that in furnishing their address details, the Post Office had printed the wrong postcode!

Finding your list

List brokers are go-betweens who source lists and assess results on your behalf. They usually earn their keep on commission from list managers and owners. (List managers market lists for list owners).

Other considerations include:

- How was the list compiled?
- Ask for a sample list print out.
- Who else had used the list and how?
- Does the list have unlimited usage or is it rented on a single-use basis?
- If your mailing is to more than 5,000, consider using a mailing house to print, package and send.
- Include your name as a 'seed' on the list to assess how long it takes to receive the mailing.
- Advise the mailing house in which order a mailing should be inserted in the envelope. (Usually letter then working 'in' to flyers and coupons). Provide a finished sample to check and print more than you need – just in case.
- Numerically code every returnable part of the mailing. This lets you keep track.
- Anticipate late deliveries.
- Check if suppliers belong to a trade organization like the Direct Marketing Association.

This time, it's personal

Whichever list you choose, where appropriate, feature a personalized name and even a different colour signature on your letters. This leaves an indelible impression of integrity as opposed to uncaring mass-mailed insincerity. According to the trade press, direct mail specifically accounts for over 12 per cent of advertising per year. Why? Simply, it is accountable. However, it also means that your mailing is competing against scores of others. It is why your mailing has to appear appealing from the envelope inwards. In *Teach Yourself Copywriting* (*see* 'Taking it Further'), I detail creative techniques to power-charge your mailings. In the meantime, it is interesting to consider some points to improve your general mailings.

Of the letters which do get opened in the morning, up to a quarter are not read until later in the day. Those which look personal and relevant are read first. Elaborate prize draw promotions are read last – if at all. The more financially biased your mailing, such as investments, insurance and banks, the less the likelihood that the mailing will be retained for future reference. This is probably down to so many companies within the financial services sector using direct mail.

Every mailing must, therefore, be carefully planned from concept to response device with maximizing return uppermost in mind. Always offer an easy method for people to contact you. Think about the sensitivity of a coupon. If you are asking for personal details, always provide a reply envelope. Don't just rely on coupons, test responses against telephone numbers, email and fax options. (Although powerful as a response device – JUST COMPLETE AND FAX BACK THIS FORM – emails are growing in popularity daily). As with all correspondence, faxes must be decent and lawful, clearly showing contact details.

Just as you invest in setting the right tone of voice and selecting the right mailing list, so offer a premium response device. By providing first-class return postage you appear serious when your brochure urges RESPOND TODAY.

Did you know?
More than 60 per cent of people read the PS part of a letter.

In telemarketing terms, opportunities are plentiful. Depending upon your budget, you can offer free calls, pay for local charges – even if the call is received at a national level. And, of course, you can provide a standard telephone number – marketed as a Hotline, Order line, Care line… and so on.

Is anybody out there?

The first indicator of a successful mailing is the extent of responses received. Many assume average response rates of around 2.5 per cent but I have found that this rate is contrived. (*See* 'Made-to-measure costs', page 73). To win greater response, look at:

- the accuracy of your data
- perceived value and relevance of your promotional offer
- scheduling of your mailing (I normally send 'anniversary' reminders no later than three months before the expiration of, say, a magazine subscription, home insurance, etc.)
- creative rationale behind your mailings contents
- creative execution of the design – especially the look, feel and copy style of the entire mailing
- ease of response.

The appeal of direct mail is that all these factors can be tested in groups or individual components. Don't assume because a mailing failed that you should re-start from scratch. Like a molecular structure, examine each element and you'll discover ample opportunities otherwise destined for the dustbin (literally).

> **Marketing in action**
> What is the difference between a list broker and list manager?

Integrated solution providers

Direct marketing isn't simply direct mail. Through a broad mix of communications, including sales promotion, press, direct response television and the Internet, direct marketing provides the appropriate conduit to 'manage' customers at every stage of the buying life cycle.

Advocate

Client

Customer

Prospects

Suspects

Through integrating appropriate media and messages, direct marketing extends a casual sale into a long-term relationship

Consumer-aware advertising

Above-the-line marketing originally referred to 'the line' above which agencies received a commission from suppliers. (Below-the-line services like sales promotion, direct mail and printing didn't pay agencies a fee.) Nowadays, through-the-line encompasses awareness media such as television, radio, the Net, cinema or publishing media. And commission is a matter of negotiation between the agency and its suppliers.

Through-the-line, integrated marketing combines above- and below-the-line marketing. Above-the-line establishes awareness; below-the-line, targets prospects directly. That requires extensive data, via lists – hence it is sometimes called database marketing.

Paying for integrated marketing

You could pay agencies a percentage of the total value of advertisements placed on your behalf but most prefer straight fees such as for design implementation and extra for disbursements like postage. (Few opt for payment by results.) Whichever route you choose, remember that if you pay below the going rate for work, agencies will be less motivated to serve than if you are 'above board'.

Integrated marketing in action

You manufacture CD and MP3 players. Advertising, perhaps on the radio, in the cinema, on television ... raises the notion that rather than someone listening to music at home, he/she could enjoy music on the move. This establishes a brand positioning which strengthens the motive that playing music on a CD player is worth pursuing. Next, you need to establish preference for your particular brand. So you further explain – by direct mail perhaps – why your CD player is particularly appropriate. Following this, you persuade the person that having opted for a CD player, yours has the edge over the competition. This could be demonstrated by a promotion through a discount or value-added campaign – a great way of dispelling any 'last minute' change of mind on the part of your customer.

Your customer buys the CD player and is happy – but it's not enough for you as an imaginative direct marketer. You want to encourage loyalty to your brand; even recommending your company to other music lovers at large. So you may follow the purchase with incentives rewarding continued allegiance. Once all done, thanks to the recommendations by your existing customers, prospects for a CD player are better targeted. Plus, in recognition of your awareness advertising, you are already further up the list of a customer's preferred brand.

> **Marketing in action**
> Organize a through-the-line media schedule for a new MP3 player.

This integrated approach adjusts itself to the age and reputation of your brand. The greater market maturity, the less need to invest in the awareness and positioning – and the greater the need to invest in loyalty (unless of course you are re-positioning your brand).

Is it a bird or a plane? – No, it's advertising!

When the citizens of Metropolis in the 1950s television series looked up and saw Superman flying, it was a visual manifestation of the 'American Way'. Similarly, advertising is the most commonly used way to pursue your imaginative strategy and make it leap up so that your audience takes note – and, hopefully, is persuaded to respond. Mass-market advertising revolves around what the *Oxford English Dictionary* describes as the most significant word of the twentieth century – *Television*.

Integrated advertising, including television marketing, doesn't have to be handled by one type of agency. Instead, integrate a compelling message, simply and clearly explained, which works creatively across every medium. In this way, the communications mix is driven by the creative proposition aiming for results rather than the channels used to feature the elementary proposition.

The more integrated your communications, the less fragmented your message

Establish desire

Draw attention to a need. *'I knew I wanted something, but until now, I didn't know what I actually needed.'*

Support it through placing your proposition in the public conscious. This often features broad awareness in television or targeted interest press. (With multi-channel digital television means that, as an integrated medium, television can be better targeted than ever). Irrespective of the medium, **deliver a singularly creative persuasive message.**

Focus on your brand

Establish an argument why your brand should be considered first. Use appropriate media such as sales leaflets and direct mail, and win brand preference.

Drive purchase

A further compelling reason to encourage a sale. *Our brand delivers more than the nearest competitor* – often features discounts and value-added promotions.

Reward loyalty

Bolster long-term and repeat purchases. This can include in-store marketing theatre (sales promotion techniques) such as, buy *this* product, get *that* one free.

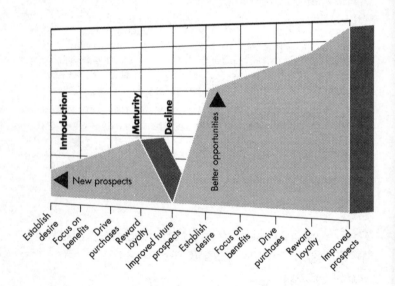

From zero to unlimited customer potential – thanks to integrated advertising

---

Marketing in action

List four considerations when selecting a direct mailing list.

14

from
e-commerce
to intelligent
commerce

In this chapter you will learn about:
- how your website can work for you
- web business benefits
- how to attract web visitors
- safe internet marketing

Andy Warhol predicted that everyone would be famous for 15 minutes. People laughed. Today, it is virtually impossible not to be filmed by closed-circuit television or become a minor celebrity in your small or wider community. You can also go into space seeing, hearing and experiencing events, right across the planet in seconds. Cyberspace (the term originally accredited to science fiction writer William Gibson) has no frontiers and unlimited potential to generate prosperity.

Despite the rise and fall of the dot coms, Cybermarketing or Internet market is arguably still the ultimate integrated marketing tool. Each day, it is estimated that thousands of new sites are added to the World Wide Web. Not only does the Web reach directly into the home, office or general environment but it captures consumer details, nurtures relationships and pulls new opportunities towards your business.

> Tremble everyone, whatever industry you are in, electronic commerce will shake you up!
>
> (*The Economist*)

Britain was once described as a nation of shopkeepers. The Internet is a continent of shops, services, conglomerates, academia, publishers – and that's the equivalent of only a single cyber high street. Electronic commerce is *Intelligent* commerce which builds then accelerates business.

Our space is your place

Initially, you may want to sell or inform via the Internet. You could build a website – or get one built. People hear about your site and so visit. This generates business which churns out information like order forms or new business leads. As your business grows, you build an Intranet – a private electronic network that 'plugs into' the Internet via a secure gateway called a Firewall (*see* 'Jargon buster', page 232). This consolidates management. Orders from around the world can now be processed directly by your accounts department. Leads can be passed on to sales people who can show, via a laptop, a web presentation of your product or service to a potential customer. On-site engineers can order parts directly from a laptop ('thin client' network computing devices – *see also* 'Jargon buster', page 235) You can monitor the general success rate of your site – including which parts are accessed the most.

Your brand builds beautifully. Casual web 'lookers' become cyber-bookers. In the tradition of classical sales promotions you can offer satisfied customers other products and services from your portfolio, selected with their proven buying preferences in mind (gained from knowledge-seeking software like Cookies).

Now you really have the competitive edge. Being digital and working via highly scaleable computer servers (which control web traffic) you no longer worry about conventional distribution issues. This alone saves money. Understandably, your managing director is pretty excited about this web venture. Following on-line research you investigate further web marketing opportunities. Your findings drive the whole process further along.

Think local – act worldwide

Let's assume your business sells event tickets for cinema, theatre, classical music performances and so on. Shows keep changing, what is 'in' this week, is 'out' next week. (The movie industry places 90 per cent of its marketing budget into the first weekend of a film premier. By Sunday night, it's usually known whether or not the movie is successful.) It's vital you get to the market quickly. Thanks to the web, within minutes, you can be first to sell tickets.

Before long, your type of marketing management gains a reputation for showing initiative. One innovation is an electronic ticket kiosk, strategically placed in the heart of town. This provides a PR launch opportunity and presents entertainment buffs with a daily reminder of your business. Using your Intranet you send to your staff an electronic newsletter about the new launch. It further bolsters team morale. (A valuable way of adding credibility with your internal customers – *see also* 'Assessing resources', page 74.)

Using the kiosk, customers select a show, swipe their credit card and pick up tickets. That calls for more web-marketing technology which electronically co-ordinates the supply of tickets from the theatre. An Extranet (external link) to suppliers enables your accounts department to co-ordinate with the credit card company who takes the opportunity to cross-market a special promotion alongside yours, mutually recruiting more customers.

The wiser world web

Network computing enables your site to be accessed via mobile phones and PCs. Being an imaginative marketer, you know that information is true power, so you design an option within your main site that records customers' enquiries and, when appropriate, sends email reminders of up-and-coming events (using Cookies). Existing customers begin to feel extra special – after all, you remembered their choice of events. This promotion 'push,' pulls in more information which can also be processed by your marketing partners. Just as the world spins so the web becomes more intricate and dynamic!

Web technology: your greatest net asset

E-branding The Internet keeps long-term brand properties fresh, original, individual and distinctive.

E-events Use your site to take registrations for events. Always aim to be innovative, for example staging on-line events, such as on-line Q and As.

E-loyalty Build and strengthen relationships by delivering privileged information over the web or use a 'push' channel to communicate and update requested information.

E-data The web offers in-depth analysis of consumer buying habits. Once you track which products or services interest consumers, data can be integrated into promotions via telemarketing or e-mail.

E-costs The web streamlines marketing costs and improves responsiveness. Updating text, introducing creative formats or launching new sales promotions can all be achieved effortlessly and quickly without expensive traditional print and production.

E-communication Integrate suppliers, employees and customers into your marketing programmes with Intranets. You can explain a campaign's overview and demonstrate how it affects your entire supply, employment and distribution chain.

E-flexibility Imagine a marketing infrastructure that scales to give your brand global coverage and handles dramatic increases in direct enquiries or orders. With scaleable hardware and software from the right partners, the networked age delivers the reality.

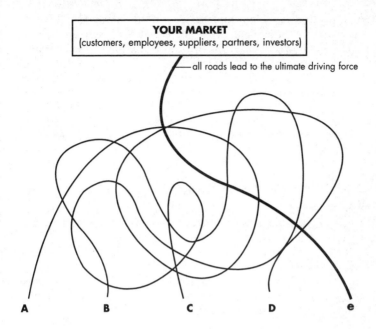

YOUR MARKET
(customers, employees, suppliers, partners, investors)

— all roads lead to the ultimate driving force

A   B   C   D   e

Now spin

When planning a website, decide first your web address – Unique
Reference Location (URL). (Also see 'Uniform Resource Locator',
page 236.) Don't confuse this with your email address. My web
address (Domain name) is *www.gabaynet.com*. It doesn't matter
how sophisticated your site, promote it wherever and whenever
you can. It builds your cyber-brand. Furthermore, don't just
provide your URL, offer a benefit. *www.gabaynet.com* doesn't tell
you anything about the company. However, a simple addition,
like a mini brand positioning statement provides greater value:

www.gabaynet.com
*– imaginative and innovative through-the-line creative
marketing solutions*

Similarly, let people know from the outset what kind of site they
are visiting – informative, business and so on. Courts of Justice
treat Domain names as intellectual property. Before you apply,
perform a web search, you could even perform a trademark
search. If you really want to protect your interests, check that
your domain name doesn't infringe rights of an established
trademark.

Next, it's time to design something. Aim for simplicity. What do you want your site to achieve? Sell, influence or perhaps become a data depot (warehouse) for stock information made accessible to your offices or mobile sales force. (Another example of Network Computing technology.) Or perhaps you want to update your customer magazine by putting it on the web. Already a significant percentage of the population has access to Interactive TV. This provides immense opportunities to marketers who want to reach a lifestyle audience watching television.

Speak everyone's language

Your commercial site will be accessed by people using different browsers and operating systems. Over 60 per cent of surfers don't have the latest browsers (Netscape Communicator or Microsoft Explorer). Therefore, use universally accessible software for new as well as older browsers. Newer applications, other than HTML such as XML and DHTML, not only bring your site to life but give access to it from the smallest palmtop to the largest mainframe system.

Designing your site

The earlier you plan your site, the better. Get yourself a roll of cheap, plain wallpaper and flow-chart your site. Start with the first page. Indicate the number of featured pages – varying text per page throughout the site. Now show links to other sites (called hypertext links). Often links are highlighted words which, when 'clicked', take the surfer on to another page. Never offer too many links per page as this may annoy surfers. Equally, never put a hypertext link in the middle of a sentence. People won't read to the end of the sentence. (Some web designers even include a flowchart of the site on the web so that surfers know where each icon leads.)

Keep the browsers on-line

Okay, you know how your site will look and what it's all about. Now watch out for pitfalls. Regularly spell-check and update your site – let surfers know when pages were last updated. Never feature a page counter. It reveals to the competition whether your site is a hit or miss. If your site is under construction, tell surfers via email to bookmark your site and let them know when it will be completed. Also email previous visitors when something new has been added. Make sure that your site can't be copied – ask your designer about this one – and check that each page of site is titled independently. Then, if someone 'hits' your site other than on the first page, they won't get lost. Another idea worth considering is to print out each page from your site. You'll be amazed by how many sites look great on screen but print blank on paper.

Wherever possible, protect the contents of your site by including a copyright notice at the foot of each page. (Never be tempted to 'lift' other people's web images; it can be illegal, so first gain permission. When possible, avoid 'clip-art' images in your design. Everyone else uses them so they can have an ill effect on brand distinction.) If you intend to sell, make sure that the terms and conditions are clear. Get the buyer to agree your terms by 'clicking' an appropriate icon.

Attracting web visitors

To market your site, first, tell the world you're on-line. This includes, advertising featuring your web address in all communications, and informing search engines like Lycos, Yahoo, Alta Vista and Google. Meta tags highlight key words about your service for the engines. If you want to go even further, place a web advert on the search engine, such as google ad words.

Further ideas to rise to the top of a web search

- Choose key subject identification words for search engines – up to three.
- Include key words – in headlines, page titles and so on.
- Only include on pages, copy and pictures which refer to your key words.
- Send search engines hypertext links (some engines can't identify images or read 'frames' and 'flash').
- Ask before offering your search engine entry. *Spamming* (see below) annoys and can be detrimental to your submission.

Did you know?
The more visually complex a web page, the slower the download time. Too slow and surfers lose interest and look elsewhere. If you have to show pictures, offer 'thumbnailed' miniatures which can be clicked and viewed in detail later. Further lengthy documentation – like industry reports – can be first summarized then offered to upload as PDFs later if requested.

What's this all about then?

All unopened sites are Pandora's boxes. Tempt surfers with trinkets to make them open yours. Maybe a free screen saver, game or even an area where other customers can 'meet' and discuss issues. (Be prepared to have someone monitor and control the 'chat area'.)

Market your site to so-called Newsgroups. These are special-interest forums. There are over 50,000 on the web (at the time of writing), so one is bound to be associated with your business. Although you can't *'spam'* – send unsolicited mail, to newsgroups or any surfers in general – as a newsgroup participant you can answer specific questions and then suggest that people may like to visit your site. (Discussion Lists are similar to newsgroups. They are much more specialized and moderators tend to filter out overt advertisements.)

There are limited email databases for rental. Also, you should market your site to on-line publications who are usually happy to accept electronic press releases. Finally you can have a free advertisement for your site. Simply include details at the bottom of your everyday emails using your ADD SIGNATURE feature which you can find as part of your Netscape or Explorer browser software.

Did you know?

An Internet Cookie is a short string of data which helps identify who's visiting your site when and which part of the site is most accessed (particularly useful for advertisers). Cookies can make a site more personalized by sending the surfer information based on previous 'hits'. Contrary to popular belief, they are not 'big brother' programs which place covert bugs into a system. If applicable you should reassure surfers that Cookies are there to help, never hinder. Cookies are great for tracking and distinguishing customers – such as paying or non-paying on-line subscribers. Yet, because of the time it would take to manage the global information, they are rarely used to capture customer data for mass mailing programmes. But, keep watching this space ...

Spread it around

One of the most significant advances in e-commerce is viral marketing – several leaps ahead of spamming. VM works because the surfer provides permission not just to receive marketing material, but also feels empowered to pass it on to fellow peers.

How safe is marketing on the Net?

Safer than you think, and you can make it even safer. When was the last time you used your credit card? Did you know that even if it wasn't swiped, someone could have jotted down your card details. On the web, he/she would have to devise a program to record your credit card details. Nowadays that's not so difficult. However, you can still make the virtual world a safer environment than the real one.

- Ask for a password which authenticates a surfer.
- Seek a digitized signature – such as one generated by Java – which proves the surfer is a bona-fide customer.
- Encrypt your data to make information impossible to read unless the person is authorized.
- Build a secure Firewall which controls and audits web access. This ensures that, once a password is accepted, surfers act as they are supposed to.

In conclusion, when on the web learn from other sites and be imaginative with yours.

15 which agency is right for you?

In this chapter you will learn about:
- how to select a communications agency
- the advantages of big vs small
- questions to pose in an agency pitch

Marketing suppliers want your money. They go to great lengths to prove no ulterior motives. One European direct marketing agency went as far as showing a picture of staff members in the nude – presumably, a vain attempt to demonstrate they had even less to hide than most! Great agencies have more to give than those claiming nothing to hide. Like all great relationships it requires a degree of give, take and, above all, trust.

An enthusiastic agency can ease your workload. You can save on costs when buying media and, of course, gain a 'buffer-zone' between you and what at times appears to be the multitude who want to sell you media, design, PR, Internet and so forth.

Just like in a personal relationship, opposites attract. Balancing strategic skills with creative know-how isn't a case of opting for an agency biased towards one or the other. Ideally, you want them to excel equally.

As in dating, ideal partnerships are usually through introduction via a mutual acquaintance. Failing this, seek recommendations from trade associations or perhaps other marketers who may well appreciate your wanting an agency that understands your needs rather than just aims for their own rewards.

Would you like an army working for you or just one specialist officer providing the same service without the extra costs to feed the troops?

The decision to opt for a large or small agency boils down to whether you want to benefit from the substantial resources available at larger companies yet remain a small fish in a large pond – or enjoy the more personal service of a smaller agency. In the latter case, agency staff members probably have a stake in the agency so will want you to be especially satisfied. However, they won't be able *directly* to offer the services of the larger agency.

Before agencies can communicate the brilliant aspects of your product or service, they have to understand more about you, where you want to be, what you offer and why someone would want to deal with you. This requires a brief, influenced by your positioning statement/platform (*see* 'Quick, what's your position on this?', page 45).

Getting an agency pitch in tune with your needs

The two-part agency audit below can be adapted according to your required communications discipline.

Part one – questions the agency should answer

- How many clients have you lost in the last three years?
- What are you proud of? – Include communication examples.
- Will the team working on the pitch also work long term on our behalf?
- How are your teams structured? What's the line of command? (Know where the 'buck stops' at each point of the communications journey.)
- What are your payment terms? Are you willing to tell us about your financial stability?
- What are your reporting procedures and what kind of a response do you expect? (This covers everyday details like paperwork. Ignore this now and you could regret it later.)
- If we can't initially decide between you and another agency, why should we choose you? (Their positioning statement.)
- Would you mind if we speak to a couple of your existing clients?

Part two – questions you should expect to be asked by an agency

- Why do you want an agency? For example, increase franchises, sell more units?... (Include organizational background notes.)
- Are you looking for only one type of communications solution? (For example, a PR proposal.)
- Which channels – including media would you consider?
- Would you consider an integrated approach?
- Do you currently use an agency? If 'YES', show recent work. If 'NO' show recent work produced 'in house'.
- How do you think your company is perceived and more importantly, how would you like it to be perceived? (This can be influenced by your mission statement, *see* page 45.)
- What justification exists for it to be perceived in that way? (Your positioning statement/platform.)

- Are you selling something – what? List three aspects that the competition either does or doesn't do any better. (Include market share, USPs, positioning and history.)
- Who are your customers? (It is not enough to say *people aged 50*. Assemble an identification kit. List interests, type of work these 'people' do, number of children, type of home...
- What do you believe these people think about your company? (Any supporting research?)
- How do you want this market to respond? (Internet, phone, mail ...)
- How much are you prepared to spend? (Agencies tend to cut the cloth to fit a wardrobe rather than suit a tailored need).
- Are there any taboos? (For example, industry regulations.)

Pay me and I'll sell you something

If you think it's right that an agency should be compensated for time, materials and labour into convincing you to place your business with them, offer a modest 'pitch fee'.

Within ten days let agencies approached know of your decision and give reasons. The choice is made and the marriage is sealed. Hopefully, the honeymoon will be the start of something great, rather than the calm before the storm. Happy hunting!

Marketing in action
Imagine you are an external agency pitching for your business. Using the Q&As above, how would you approach the project?

6

sales and marketing – made for each other

In this chapter you will learn about:
- sales principles
- Kudzu™ selling
- how to negotiate

There is no such thing as selling, just helping

Imagine taking a prospective buyer out for lunch. Seated at the table are the customer, a salesperson and yourself. The object is to persuade the customer to buy a new car. Your imaginative marketing campaign details strategic issues like the car's brand positioning and USPs. It all helps to establish credibility in the buyer's mind. But it doesn't secure a sale.

The salesperson develops a tactical one-to-one relationship with the prospective buyer. The salesperson can be compared to the buyer's best friend who knows inside facts that you don't, such as the buyer's rival has recently bought a top-of-the-range model from a competitive manufacturer. So when the salesperson approaches the buyer, it is from a position of the prospective customer's self-worth.

So it is that marketing and sales should work in unity. Instead of marketing simply being a department that produces literature and sales being a force driven by targets rather than market awareness, the two work as a team, each undertaking a complementary role.

Beacon Group, a world leading provider of management analysis and planning systems (MAPS) has devised the following set of powerful sales principles:

The Beacon Sales Principles

1 Listen

2 Add value to your customer's life – Remember that your customer has a customer. In the case of buying a car, those customers may include a spouse and children. So your sales techniques must adapt and so demonstrate how he/she can justify to them buying a more expensive car.

3 Ensure your customer perceives a 'win–win' scenario. He/she must not feel vulnerable or that you have been left vulnerable. No one gets a sour deal and so the sale becomes the start of an all-round profitable partnership.

4 A sale does not finish when a contract is signed or you get paid. The first sale always costs more than the sales which follow. Aim to develop this cost-effective route.

5 Give valued customers your home telephone number. It creates trust and stops you from being just a sales person but makes you a valued personal contact.

Can you really win–win?

There are two approaches to sales negotiation – 'win at all costs (WAAC)' and 'win–win (WW)'. The WAAC negotiator sees every negotiation as a struggle between winning and losing.

WAAC negotiators:
• Initially take extreme positions
• Claim limited authority, so you end up bidding against yourself rather than them!
• Manipulate emotional tactics
• From the outset treat you as an adversary
• View any concessions you make as weaknesses
• Offer limited concessions
• Miss deadlines.

Your options here are to:

• Beat them at their own game with the same tactics
• Walk away
• Try a collaborative 'win–win' approach

WW negotiators:
• Aim to produce acceptable gains for all parties
• View conflicts as problems to be solved
• See conflicts as opportunities to be more creative, thus enhancing positions
• See relationships as being based on respect and trust.

Kudzu selling™

'Never give up' is key to successful selling. After all, if pioneers had listened to their critics, Columbus would never have discovered America, man would never have gone to the moon and you wouldn't take that important step in your own life... In fact, all potentials would be halted. It takes imagination and perseverance to succeed. Yet endurance is not enough. To be adaptable, you must have vision to see opportunities where others are short-sighted. I call this Kudzu selling™. *Kudzu* was introduced to the south-eastern United States in 1876. It is a vine native to Japan and can grow 45 cm (18 inches) a day – up to 30 metres (100 feet) in a single growing season. Kudzu has sprouted its own industry comprising anything from kudzu jelly to poetry devoted to the vine. As a salesperson you have to be equally tenacious, getting to the roots of a project, covering every detail to finding new ways to reach customers and extend values to existing clients. By listening to your prospect's views before 'jumping in' with a sales proposition, you can negotiate a better solution for you, your client and the company. This turns a win–lose sales exercise into a win–win standard.

Remember, *life's a pitch – and then you buy!* More sales tips are covered in detail in *Teach Yourself Selling*. (Note to Editor – please send me a cheque for my sales commission on this recommendation!)

17

the future. it's in your hands

In this chapter you will learn about:
- what the future might hold for marketing professionals
- how the future might affect the six Ps
- issues for the twenty-first century

Your world is changing. A marketing job with one company is no longer for life. Instead, your career encompasses many amazing facets. Technology continues to shift market demands. Micro-chips halve in size and double in capacity every 18 months. Therefore logically, information technology will eventually destroy its own digital age to be replaced by crystal storage, photonics then nanotechnology. Information will be incorporated into chromosomes within DNA cells. Imagine, you'll target people using neural marketing programmes accessed by thought alone.

Place – distribution cycles will be further reduced through borderless currency, telecommunications and working communities. **Promotion** – campaigns will be more precision targeted. **Price** – less bulky production materials will drive down costs. **Processes** – will become more dependent on thinking and design rather than actualization, the easy part. **Physical evidence** will bring brands to 'life' through value added consumer experiences which constantly adapt. **People** – will, once again, take centre stage, shaping, managing and manipulating the market.

By the mid twenty-first century, the focus will be on issues over data protection and direct access to personal neural networks. Looking further, as the world's population swells and we colonise other planets, so marketing will become even more advanced. Dispersed cliques may connect their minds to brand 'lifestyle spheres' where a brand's values come to life in a virtual setting. (*See also* 'Virtual brainstorming', page 137).

Mineral resources on our planet will naturally decrease, yet humankind's natural intellectual resources will be developed to replenish and make what we have go further. The most valued currency will be imagination. The strategy to communicate will continue to be marketing and the market, as always, will create demand to be satisfied by the enterprising few.

However technologically advanced we become, I hope that by acting as your guide around the world of marketing I have demonstrated that every marketing tool supports just one thing – stimulating ways to deal with people – profitably.

However far you venture in your own career, right now, you have the power to change your world and the community around you. It doesn't matter whether you are part of a conglomerate or marketing on your own. It takes only a single idea and persuasive method to kindle the imaginative spirit.

It's a big market out there – Go and conquer it!

g

jj@gabaynet.com

appendix

Typical marketing production times

Brochure, including copy, print and design	Six weeks
Business cards	Ten days
Christmas cards	One month
Corporate ID	Six weeks–four months Three months–seven months (international)
Direct mail, including copy and design	Four weeks
Newsletters including copy, design and print	Four weeks
Overhead presentation material	One week
Press advertisement – design, copy, photography and placement	Six weeks
Press release	One–seven days
Radio commercial (including planning and production)	One day–ten days
Re-branding	Seven–ten months
TV commercial or corporate video (including planning and production)	Seven weeks–four months
Website, including copy, design and planning	Four months

NB: Always treat a written brief as a legal contract. Never accept to undertake a marketing project without a satisfactory brief which is agreed and signed by all parties.

Speak easy – jargon buster

advertising effectiveness targeted audience recall of an advertising message

advertising funded media funded totally or partly from advertising

Advertising Standards Authority promotes and enforces the highest standards in non-broadcast advertisements in the UK and acts independently of the government and advertising industry

advocacy advertising corporate advertising highlighting a company's position on a mission-critical question

affinity marketing joint sponsorship by broadly un-competitive businesses sharing a common interest in an event (e.g. the soccer World Cup)

'affordable' method advertising budget based upon what can be afforded, rather than needs to be achieved

'arbitrary' method advertising budget which doesn't consider basic calculations or even the desired result

arena advertising posters seen at an event as well as wider television audience

ASDL Asymmetric Digital Subscriber Line; transmits digital information at high speed

Audit Bureau of Circulation provides the UK's independent system for the validation of circulation and exhibition data

back-to-back commercials broadcast within the same commercial break for the same product or pair of complementary products/ services

BBS web bulletin board system

behavioural intent following a marketing programme, customer's perception awareness and ultimately intent to purchase a product or service

best practice an exceptional style of service and process which makes a company perceived as being top in its class

bitmap dots on web page which make up a picture

biz web newsgroup which discusses commercial issues

Blitzkrieg advertising see **fast marketing**

BOGOFF mnemonic for Buy One Get One Free, i.e. 2 for the price of 1 promotions

bottom-up planning plans and suggestions which form an integrated corporate plan. Opposite – **top-down planning**

brand conditioning campaign which complements a brand impression

Brand Manager (aka Product Manager) executive who controls a specific brand's marketing communications

brand properties collective features which shape a brand's personality

brand reinforcement support for customers' beliefs and so disposition towards a brand

brand share percentage of a brand's sales/consumption sales rather than total market. Calculations are based on either levels of units sold, distributed, income or general awareness

browser a program which enables you to see web pages

calling cycle average duration between calls to a specific customer

canned presentation standard sales or marketing presentation committed to memory

cognitive dissonance conflicting ideas and actions (e.g. buying something which normally you would never purchase)

commando selling intensive campaign into a new market with a new product or service using a specially recruited sales force

culture relates to either corporate or consumer beliefs, values and behaviour

customized marketing tailored as opposed to mass-marketed services or products

CUT Consumer Usage Test

cyber-brand brand developed via the Internet

cyber-marketing web-centric marketing

DAR Day After Recall (market research)

decay effect the result of a brand being forgotten because of lack of marketing

diadic two people separately reporting findings on two advertisements or products

dirty proof proof full of amendments

dissonance reduction theory a person's need for convincing that a product or service is worth buying

divergent marketing separate organizations within a company with individual marketing goals and profit centres

domain official Internet address

dumping products sold and distributed overseas for less than they would be marketed locally

dynamically continuous same service or product but technically enhanced to be re-marketed for a new audience

electronic catalogue accessible web site database, featuring products or services, leading to electronic shopping

electronic shopping sales via the web

end values a person's most important values – love, security, welfare…

end-user the consumer who actually uses rather than pays for a product or service

Engel's Law theory which suggests that as a person's income increases by the percentage of that income spent on food decreases

EPOs Electronic Point of Sale

equivalent advertising value sum total of publicity and editorial coverage in the press, in terms of space, compared to buying the equivalent space using advertising

ethical advertising advertising aimed at the medical profession. Also describes honest as opposed to deceitful advertising

events marketing campaign which invites customers or prospects to a venue

family life cycle
    a) Young, alone living outside parental home.
    b) Just married/co-habitating, no children.
    c) Married/co-habiting, youngest child under six.
    d) Married/co-habiting, youngest child over six.
    e) Married/co-habiting, child about to become independent.
    f) Children left home, breadwinner still in employment.
    g) Children left home, breadwinner retired.
    h) Surviving partner is the breadwinner.
    i) Surviving partner is retired.

fast marketing aka **Blitzkrieg advertising**: advertising delivered at once over a relatively short timescale to encourage a high-volume response

flanking attack ambushing a competitor at a weak spot

filler pre-prepared advertisement to be used as a last minute 'filler' in the press – often published at cut cost

Firewall an installed and connected computer (or several) between an Intranet and Internet controlling user access

first proof initial proof of promotional material to check for spelling or other errors

flag a chosen person highlighted within a database for future testing or re-mailing

flashpack packaging with a sales promotion message

free continuous premium coupons redeemed for a gift or concession according to the number of purchases

gable end poster at the end wall of a building

generic products un-branded products aimed at frugal customers

generic term brand name to describe a type of product (e.g. Hoover, Xerox)

gestation period elapsed time between an initial product inquiry and order

government relations PR dealing with local, national and international interests

guerrilla marketing attacks competitive activities through confusion and demoralisation techniques with the aim to capture a niche spot in the market

Hall test research technique also known as *In-Theatre Research*, in which people at a specific location answer questions for a marketing campaign

hidden value initially insignificant value which is later promoted by a supplier

homepage your main web page

housewife time the radio broadcast period between morning rush hour and the early evening drive times

HTML Hypertext Mark-up Language – basic language for writing web pages

hypertext highlighted text on a web site displaying further information or making a complementary website connection when 'clicked' with a mouse

incentive marketing added incentives such as prize draws and discount vouchers

in-home media any media in the home (e.g. television, lifestyle press, radio and Web TV)

in-home use test pre-product testing in consumer's home

institutional advertising advertising for entire sectors (e.g. It's safe to eat British Beef)

institutional market community care market – hospitals, schools, prisons

intelligent agent web software which searches the web for information based on your preferences

Internet relay chat a web system which enables surfers to see and hear each other in real time

ISDN Integrated Services Digital Network (for speeding up the production process between studio and printer). *See also* ASDL.

Java a language and platform for distributed network computing

joint promotion a co-sponsored and managed promotion aimed at increasing impact whilst reducing marketing costs

key success factor the essential element which makes a product or service a market success

killer application 'must have' software (e.g. email)

law of demand the higher the price, the lower the demand (or vice versa)

letterbox marketing hand-distributed marketing promotions – usually with free local newspapers

live marketing management of any situation where a customer interacts face to face with a brand, ensuring a positive brand perception

loyalty marketing brand loyalty programme featuring gifts/financial incentives

lumpy demand lumps in demand due to seasonal variations of consumer tastes

MAPS Management Analysis and Planning Systems; designed for the measurement and control of critical business functions

market reach the maximum number of prospects reached with a marketing campaign

market recognition common brand or product awareness usually gauged in percentage sales

micro marketing marketing tailored to address individual objectives

mood advertising advertising which instils an attitude conducive to a product or service

NABS the only major UK charity that covers the whole of the marketing communications industry

neck hanger a sales promotion device like a miniature leaflet affixed to the neck of a bottle

new media multimedia such as the World Wide Web, DVDs, Digital TV and CD-ROMS

nixies undeliverable addresses

noise over-exposed advertising messages to a wearied audience

on-line anything performed whilst connected to the web

pass-on readership total readership of a publication, including those who didn't actually buy it in the first place (**tertiary readership** – read publication casually whilst sitting in a waiting room e.g. at the dentist)

penetration pricing a cut-price strategy to gain quick, wide market penetration

plug-ins web software to run value-added programs such as audio or video

product clutter outdated products which hinder innovative marketing management

professional services marketing marketing aimed at professionals such as lawyers, accountants and architects

push technology digitally 'pushing' information based on a consumer's preferences through a computer and thereby creating a tailored, value-added sales channel

quasi retailing retailers selling things apart from core products (e.g. building societies, funeral parlours, hotels)

quota sample pre-selected research groups, representative of the larger population

readership profile segmentation of readership

rears advertising spaces on the back of cars, taxis, buses and trams

repositioning a campaign to alter perceived brand values and relevance

rifle approach a targeted message at a targeted audience; opposite – **blunderbuss approach**

sales impact measurement of sales activities

sales platform main sales proposition

salting aka Seeding, or Sleeper; name within a mailing list who monitors the mailing process

search engine an electronic web page location indexing system

semi-solus advertisement which appears on the same page as another – but not next to it

share of voice percentage of your marketing budget compared to your competitors'

SKU Stock Keeping Units (goods on superstore shelves)

SLP Self Liquidating Promotion (pays for itself)

starch ratings US advertising effectiveness measurement system

suit slang for marketing or advertising, account administrator, manager or director

tactical pricing price manipulation to encourage sales

TAP Total Audience Package – broadcast spots stretched out over time

TAT Thematic Apperception Test – consumers artistically describing feelings about a product or service with pen and paper

teaser intriguing advertisement such as a poster or direct mailer

thin client a computer terminal which performs the functions of a PC but accesses application software from a network rather than storing it on hard disk

tissue first-draft creative concepts presentation

top-of-mind easily recalled brand – not necessarily the brand leader

torture test to demonstrate endurance, a product or service is subjected to extremes

unaided brand awareness number of a research sample who can name a brand after summarizing similar products or services within a sector

undifferentiated marketing technique mass marketing without any distinctive target audience benefits

universe selection of population used as a research sample

URL Uniform Resource Locator – expresses the location of a web page

vehicle medium featured in a marketing communications programme

vertical market services or products segmented within a single market classification

video on demand videos, such as those used in promotions, stored on a central server and run on request, exclusively for an individual via a PC, network computing device or television

viral marketing encouragement of market to 'push' a marketing message throughout a community, and in doing so enhance their reputation within communities that interact with each other

virtual agency network creative suppliers collaborating to provide a marketing communications service either nationally or globally

voucher copy complimentary magazine – usually to see a published advertisement in situ

waste circulation percentage of published circulation which has no value to a marketer but still needs to be paid for

webcasting broadcasting over the Internet

white goods consumer durables such as microwave ovens, fridges and washing machines

wobbler adhesive sales promotion display device which 'wobbles' when touched

X-bar statistical symbol which represents an average

X-factor the inexact marketing aspect within a person or a company that can't be copied but equals success

YES bias a respondent's tendency to complete the YES boxes in a coupon

Z-card miniature brochure folded into a credit-card sized format

Z-chart a chart showing values over a period of time such as a year whilst providing daily, weekly or monthly figures to support the sum total

zone plan marketing test for a new product or service using advertising in a highly targeted, small geographic area

Useful contacts

United Kingdom

AC Tucker & Co (Marketing accountancy specialists)
email: stucker@dircon.co.uk

Advertising Association
www.adassoc.org.uk

Advertising Standards Authority
www.asa.org.uk
Copy rules advice on advertising and promotions
Tel: +44 (0)20 7580 4100

Audit Bureau of Circulation
www.abc.org.uk

Beacon Group
info@beaconit.com.au

British Market Research Association (BMRA)
www.bmra.org.uk

Broadcast Advertising Clearance Centre
www.bacc.com.uk

Broadcasters' Audience Research Board
Tel: +44 (0)20 7741 9110

Broadcasting Standards Council
Tel: +44 (0)20 7233 0544

Chartered Institute of Marketing
www.cim.co.uk

Clearwater Communications
www.clearwater.co.uk

Communication, Advertising and Marketing Foundation (CAM) Ltd
www.cam.uk.com

Creative Interpartners
ci@creativeinterpartners.co.uk

The Creativity Works
www.theworks.co.uk

Design Council
www.design-council.org.uk

Direct Marketing Association
www.dma.org.uk

Gabay – Marketing resources including education
www.gabaynet.com

Guy Facey – Amhurst Brown Colombotti
guy.facey@abc-solicitors.com

Henley Centre
Tel: +44 (0)20 7878 3186

ICSTIS (The Independent
Committee for the
Supervision of Standards
of Telephone
Information Services)
Tel: +44 (0)20 7240 5511
(Offers a free checking service
for copy written for use over
premium rate telephone lines.)
(Complaints about premium
rate telephone lines, call 0800
500 212.)
www.icstis.org.uk/

Incorporated Society of British
Advertisers
www.isba.org.uk

Independent Television
Commission
www.itc.org.uk

Institute of Direct Marketing
www.thidm.co.uk

Institute of Directors
www.iod.co.uk

The Institute of Packaging
www.info@iop.co.uk

Institute of Practitioners in
Advertising (IPA)
www.ipa.co.uk

Institute of Public Relations
www.ipr.press.net

Institute of Sales Promotion
(ISP and SPCA)
www.isp.org.uk.

Mailing Preference Service
www.dma.org.uk

Market Research Society
www.marketresearch.org.uk

The Marketing Society
email: info@marketing-
society.org.uk

NABS
32 Wigmore Street,
London
W1H 9DF
Tel: +44 (0)20 7299 2888
www.nabs.org.uk

The Newspaper Society
www.newspapersoc.org.uk

NOP Research Group
Tel: +44 (0)20 7890 9439
email: T.lees@nopres.co.uk

Oracle
www.oracle.com

Public Relations Consultants
Association
www.prca.org.uk

SRI International
Tel: +44 (0)20 7446 6166

Sun Microsystems
www.sun.co.uk

The Netherlands

Esomar
www.esomar.nl

Australia

The Advertising Institute
of Australia
Adelaide
Fax: +61 8 21 21 238

Australian Association of
National Advertisers
Sydney
Tel: +61 2 9221 8088

Australian Direct Marketing
Association Ltd
Sydney
Tel: +61 2 247 7744

Australian Federation of
  Advertising
North Sydney
Tel: +61 2 957 3077

Australian Marketing Institute
Melbourne
Tel: +61 3 820 8788

Council of Sale Promotional
  Agencies
Tel: +61 203 325 3911

Public Relations Institute of
  Australia (New South Wales)
North Sydney
Tel: +61 2 369 2029

Public Relations Institute
  of Australia
Tel: +61 2 369 2029

PRIA (Queensland)
Tel: +61 7 368 3662

PRIA (South Australia)
Marden South Australia 5070
Tel: +61 8 362 1559

PRIA (Tasmania)
Tel: +61 0 233 4439

PRIA (Victoria)
PO Box 21
Hawthorn Victoria 3122

PRIA (Western Australia)
East Perth
Tel: +61 9 421 7555

Promotion Industry Club (Sales)
Naperville
Tel: +61 708 369 3772

Canada

Canadian Direct Marketing
  Association
Toronto, Ontario
Tel: +1 416 391 2362

Canadian Public Relations
  Society Inc. (CPRS)
Ottawa, Ontario
Tel: +1 613 232 122

Institute of Canadian
  Advertising
Toronto, Ontario
Tel: +1 416 482 1396

United States

Advertising Council Inc.
New York
Tel: +1 212 922 1500

American Advertising
  Federation
Washington DC
Tel: +1 202 898 0089

American Association of
  Advertising Agencies
New York
Tel: +1 212 682 2500

American Marketing
  Association
Chicago
Tel: +1 312 648 0536

Business Professional
  Advertising
  Association
Alexandria VA
Tel: +1 703 683 2722

Direct Marketing Association
New York
Tel: +1 212 768 7277

International Advertising
  Association
New York
Tel: +1 212 557 1133

Marketing Research
  Association
Connecticut
Tel: +1 203 257 4008

Point-of-Purchase Advertising
   Institute
Englewood NJ
Tel: +1 201 894 8899

Public Relations Society
   of America
New York
Tel: +1 212 995 2230

Hong Kong

Public Relations Association of
   Hong Kong Limited
(PRAHK)
GPO Box 1264
Hong Kong

Further recommended reading

Reinvent Yourself by J. Jonathan Gabay, Momentum, 2002,
ISBN 18403040158
Successful Cybermarketing in a Week by J. Jonathan Gabay,
Hodder Headline, 2000
Teach Yourself Copywriting by J. Jonathan Gabay, Hodder &
Stoughton, 2003 ISBN 0-340-86728-0
Trade Name Origins – NTC Publishing Group, ISBN 0-8442-
0904-X

Recommended marketing courses

Chartered Institute of Marketing
www.cim.co.uk

Institute of Direct Marketing
Tel: +44 (0)20 8977 5705

Institute of Sales Promotion
Tel: +44 (0)20 7837 5340

Further learning

www.gabaynet.com

index

teach
yourself

setting up a small business
vera hughes & david weller

- Are you setting up a small business?
- Do you need help to define your product or service?
- Are you looking for guidance in marketing and finance?

Setting Up a Small Business helps you with all the everyday aspects of running a small business and gives detailed guidance on specialised areas such as legal requirements, opening a retail or office-based business, staff selection and marketing.

Vera Hughes and **David Weller** started their own business in 1980, having been involved in the retail industry for many years. They have written a number of books on retailing.

e-commerce
neil denby

- Does your small business need an e-commerce facility?
- Are you planning an Internet start-up?
- Do you want to learn more about the benefits and pitfalls of e-commerce?

E-Commerce provides a simple explanation of e-business, with practical guidance on setting up a website. Hints and tips, a glossary and useful weblinks make this an essential guide to an ever-changing subject.

Neil Denby is a university lecturer in business, economics and education and a successful business author.

teach yourself

presenting for professionals
phil baguley and janet bateman

- Do you have to give impressive presentations?
- Do you want your presentations to hit the spot every time?
- Do you need to move your presenting up a gear?

Presenting for Professionals will enable you to give presentations that are powerful, passionate, persuasive and, above all, professional. It covers the how, why, what and when of presenting in a way that's never been done before. It's rich in practical tips, jam-packed with insider advice and big on multimedia know-how.

Phil Baguley is a business writer who has held senior management roles in multinational corporations. **Janet Bateman** has extensive experience in training and personal development.